Read and Think!

A Reading Strategies Course

Teacher's Manual

Ken Beatty

Published by
Longman Asia ELT
2/F Cornwall House
Taikoo Place
979 King's Road
Quarry Bay
Hong Kong

fax: +852 2856 9578
email: pearsonlongman@pearsoned.com.hk
www.longman.com

and Associated Companies throughout the world.

First published 2004
Reprinted 2006
Produced by Pearson Education Asia Limited, Hong Kong
EPC/03

ISBN-13: 978-962-01-8402-4
ISBN-10: 962-01-8402-5

Design Manager: Winnie Sung
Editor: Hoi Kin Chiu
Designer: Waimann Lee
Illustrators: Brian Wan, Waimann Lee

We are grateful to Corbis for permission to reproduce copyright photographs.

The publisher's policy is to use **paper manufactured from sustainable forests**

Contents

Introduction

Getting the most out of *Read and Think!*

Take a moment to put yourself in the place of a student learning to read English at a secondary school or higher level. You probably studied English for many years and the experience is likely to have been mixed: some good times and some bad times.

In the worst cases, the purpose for learning to read has not been for the best of reasons. Instead of enjoyment, reading in English is probably most closely identified with complicated tests that seem to have been engineered for the purpose of "tricking" you. Often the content of the readings has not been interesting, especially in older books with topics twenty years out of date filled with vocabulary seldom used outside a classroom.

Such experiences don't motivate students to want to improve their reading.

Read and Think! is a series that turns reading into a positive, interesting experience. Most good readers know that reading is enormously enjoyable, a door to a wide world of information and entertainment. Good readers also know that reading is much more than simply knowing the meaning of a series of words; it's a process of discovery.

In fact, reading can be described as detective work in which a good reader uses a series of tools to solve problems and understand ideas.

Read and Think! is written by a teacher for teachers. The purpose of the series is to help your students see reading as an interesting problem-solving activity. Through the use of a variety of text types with carefully integrated graphics, the series aims to improve students' reading skills. The different readings cover issues important to university students, including ethical and academic issues.

The series

The four Student Books each offer twelve units of two lessons each.

Level 1: 250–300 words per reading
Level 2: 300–400 words per reading
Level 3: 600–700 words per reading
Level 4: 800+ words per reading

Components in the Student Book

Unit content

Each unit of ***Read and Think!*** begins with a title and keywords taken from general fields of study, usually university disciplines.

Lesson One

- **Before you read** starts off with questions that encourage students to think about the topic of the unit. As a warm-up activity, have students discuss the questions in pairs, small groups or as a class. A picture, map, diagram or illustration follows with something for students to do, think about or discuss. Use this to create more interest in the topic and explore new vocabulary.
- **Read about it** takes students into the first of the unit's two readings. Before they start reading, ask students to listen with their books closed. Two questions before each reading give students something to think about when they listen. Students should then read the passage on their own. Finally, students read and listen together to match pronunciation with comprehension. **Vocabulary notes** from the *Longman Active Study Dictionary* help students learn and understand keywords from the reading.
- **After you read** gives students a chance to show what they know by answering questions about the reading. The **Reading strategy** section provides important information to help students get more out of what they read. This includes explanations and tips that are followed up in an exercise. Other

exercises such as fill-in-the-blanks give students extra reading and comprehension practice. A **What about you?** section helps students see their own place in the topic.

Lesson Two

- **Read about it** offers a second reading to give another perspective on the unit topic to help students think about what they read. Sometimes these second readings take the opposite point of view. The section begins with discussion questions for students to think about while listening to the passage. Listening before reading gives students a chance to listen for the gist or key points. **Vocabulary notes** from the *Longman Active Study Dictionary* help students learn keywords from the reading.
- **After you read** has a higher level task, such as summarizing a paragraph in one sentence, as well as fun activities, such as word puzzles. This is followed by multiple choice comprehension questions.
- **Debate** gives students a chance to show what they know by arguing a point based on the unit topic. Two perspectives on the same idea are given with supporting points and room for students to add their own ideas. **Another idea to debate** expands the unit topic to provide students with a related idea for further discussion or debate.
- **Learn more** gives students a chance to discover more about the unit topic and report their findings to the class.
- **Look online** directs students to the ***Read and Think!*** companion website at www.read-and-think.com for extra learning resources.

Features

- **Strategies** and **notes** throughout the unit provide students with information and tips about reading, language, culture, computer usage, debates and exams.
- A collection of all **Exam strategies** mentioned throughout the book can be found on page 143.
- **Debate strategies** mentioned throughout the book are listed on pages 144–145.
- A **Skills check** on page 142 allows students to assess and reflect on what they have learned in each unit.
- A **Personal dictionary** on page 146 provides space for students to write their own dictionary, adding unfamiliar words as they encounter them.
- Students can record all their readings in the **Personal reading diary** on page 147, as well as time their readings and record their speeds on the table on page 143.

Other *Read and Think!* components

- All readings are recorded on the CD by native English speakers. Students can listen for correct pronunciation and intonation.
- Further assessment is available through the CD-ROM Test Bank, which can be used to create photocopy masters.
- The website at www.read-and-think.com offers further teacher and student support.

Unit 1

The Search for Atlantis

Fields of study

Each unit begins with a knowledge base taken from general subject areas. In Unit 1, the subjects are **Geography**, **Philosophy** and **Mythology**. Ask students what they know about these subjects. A good general activity is to ask students *why* people study each subject.

Possible answers are:

- Geography teaches us about the relationships of people and things across space. It is a useful tool for examining changes and differences.
- Philosophy explores the great questions in life, such as why we are here and what we should do with our lives.
- Mythology explores ancient stories, many of which are important to understanding human nature.

Lesson One

Background information

This unit deals with aspects of Greek and Roman civilizations. These are important to understanding modern-day Western countries. The philosophies, teachings, legal and governing systems and even the Roman alphabet helped shape Western civilization. Understanding more about Greek and Roman civilizations is a quick way of understanding more about the modern world.

Before you read

The questions in this section give you a chance to elicit background knowledge from students and to create interest in the unit topic. At this point, don't worry about getting all the correct answers. It can be more useful to write on the board what students think and refer back to their answers later to show them how much they have learned after completing the lesson.

Encourage students to share extra knowledge they have on the topic.

The Search for Atlantis

UNIT 1

Geography
Philosophy
Mythology

Lesson One

discussion

Before you read

- What did this structure look like when it was new?
- What was it used for?

Why do you think this building was allowed to fall apart?

Ruins in Greece

1

Answers

- When it was new, the structure was made up of two sets of columns like background. They were set in a double circle and would have been covered by a dome. In the center might have been a pool of water or well.
- The structure was originally used as a temple for religious ceremonies. The temple is known as *Tholos Temple, a Sanctuary of Athena at Delphi*. A *tholos* was sometimes used as a tomb.

Why do you think this building was allowed to fall apart?

It may have fallen apart and the people who could fix it were no longer around. It may have been destroyed in a war.

Look at the picture(s) at the beginning of the unit. Most units begin with an activity related to the picture. If there isn't one, ask students to describe the picture on a factual level, but also give their impressions about it. Encourage students to think of questions about the picture and answer them. Use questions beginning with *who, what, when, where, why* and *how*. For example, in this unit, we could ask the question, "Why has this structure been allowed to fall apart?" Answers might include the fact that it is extremely old and the religion that once was important there faded away.

Read about it

It's best if students listen once with books closed then listen again with books opened. Adjust this depending on the level of your class and encourage students to listen again on their own. Listening and reading at the same time helps teach pronunciation. As students listen, they should try to think of the answers to the two questions and check their answers as they read a second or third time.

Encourage students to keep a record of their reading speeds on the table on page 143 of the Student Book.

> **Answers**
> - The city of Atlantis is "lost" for two reasons: first, because it was supposedly destroyed by an earthquake and sank into the sea and, second, because there is no record of where it once stood. People continue to search for it.
> - This question is meant to make students listen for emphasis in capitals, names, places and the first words of sentences.

As a follow-up activity, ask some of the more able students to read the passage aloud.

Encourage students to record their readings in the personal reading diary on page 147 of the Student Book.

Where Is the Lost City?

This reading explains the origins of the story, or myth, of Atlantis. It also introduces Plato and Socrates and the idea of the Academy, the model for modern universities. Most people agree that Atlantis is a mythical city that was described as a way of discussing philosophical arguments about good government. The fact that it is most likely a myth has not stopped people from looking for it for centuries.

The first paragraph introduces Atlantis. The second paragraph traces the origin of the story, suggesting Atlantis was an example of a point of debate. The third paragraph tells more about Atlantis and the fourth paragraph raises the question of where we might find Atlantis—if it ever actually existed.

Language note

Review the language note, making sure students understand the general idea.

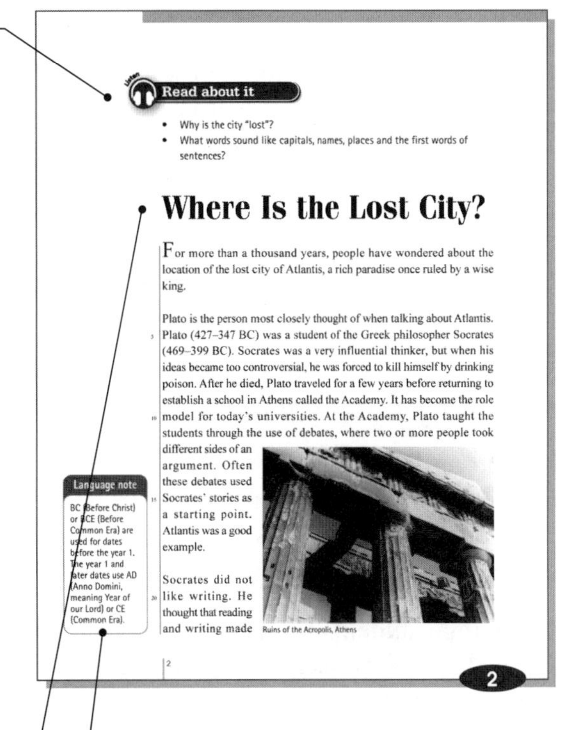

Read about it

- Why is the city "lost"?
- What words sound like capitals, names, places and the first words of sentences?

Where Is the Lost City?

For more than a thousand years, people have wondered about the location of the lost city of Atlantis, a rich paradise once ruled by a wise king.

Plato is the person most closely thought of when talking about Atlantis. Plato (427–347 BC) was a student of the Greek philosopher Socrates (469–399 BC). Socrates was a very influential thinker, but when his ideas became too controversial, he was forced to kill himself by drinking poison. After he died, Plato traveled for a few years before returning to establish a school in Athens called the Academy. It has become the role model for today's universities. At the Academy, Plato taught the students through the use of debates, where two or more people took different sides of an argument. Often these debates used Socrates' stories as a starting point. Atlantis was a good example.

Socrates did not like writing. He thought that reading and writing made

Language note: BC (Before Christ) or BCE (Before Common Era) are used for dates before the year 1. The year 1 and later dates use AD (Anno Domini, meaning Year of our Lord) or CE (Common Era).

Ruins of the Acropolis, Athens

2

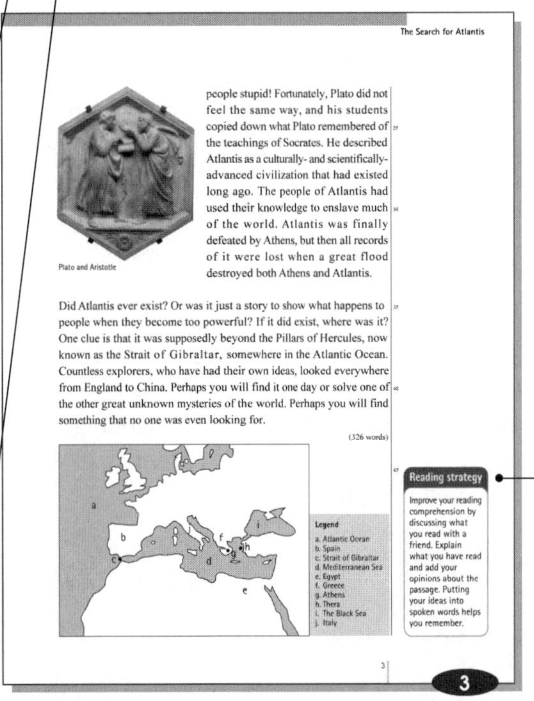

The Search for Atlantis

people stupid! Fortunately, Plato did not feel the same way, and his students copied down what Plato remembered of the teachings of Socrates. He described Atlantis as a culturally- and scientifically-advanced civilization that had existed long ago. The people of Atlantis had used their knowledge to enslave much of the world. Atlantis was finally defeated by Athens, but then all records of it were lost when a great flood destroyed both Athens and Atlantis.

Plato and Aristotle

Did Atlantis ever exist? Or was it just a story to show what happens to people when they become too powerful? If it did exist, where was it? One clue is that it was supposedly beyond the Pillars of Hercules, now known as the Strait of Gibraltar, somewhere in the Atlantic Ocean. Countless explorers, who have had their own ideas, looked everywhere from England to China. Perhaps you will find it one day or solve one of the other great unknown mysteries of the world. Perhaps you will find something that no one was even looking for.

(326 words)

Legend: a. Atlantic Ocean; b. Spain; c. Strait of Gibraltar; d. Mediterranean Sea; e. Egypt; f. Greece; g. Athens; h. Thera; i. The Black Sea; j. Italy

Reading strategy: Improve your reading comprehension by discussing what you read with a friend. Explain what you have read and add your opinions about the passage. Putting your ideas into spoken words helps you remember.

3

Reading strategy

Review the reading strategy, making sure students understand the general idea. Refer back to these strategies from time to time to make sure students are using them.

Vocabulary notes

Review the vocabulary notes, making sure students can use the words in sentences and different contexts. As an easy bonus activity at the end of class, give a spelling test based on these words. The *Longman Active Study Dictionary* is a companion dictionary recommended to accompany Level 2 of *Read and Think!* All the key vocabulary in the Student Book is clearly defined in this dictionary, which is at an appropriate level for students using this book.

Reading strategy

Review the reading strategy, making sure students understand the general idea.

Add new words

Encourage students to keep a record of new words they encounter and add them to a list at the back of the Student Book on page 146.

Read and listen again

This gives students another opportunity to connect the written text to how it is pronounced at both the word and sentence level.

After you read

A. Answer these questions.

This section offers comprehension questions to help students think more deeply about what they have read. Review these questions before students read. Encourage students to answer in full sentences and think carefully of any other answers that might be possible.

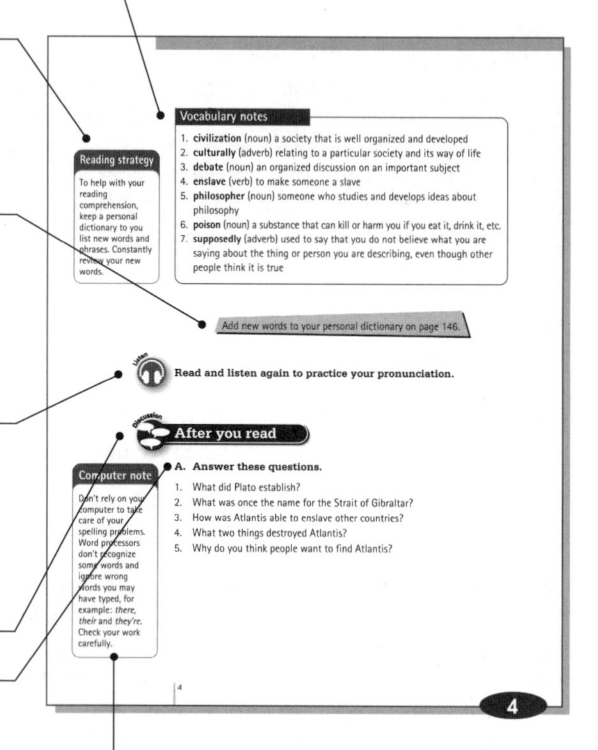

Computer note

Many students do much of their writing and reading on computers. It is important that they use the computer effectively as a tool for learning. Review the computer note, making sure students understand the general idea.

Answers

1. Plato established the Academy, the model for modern universities.
2. A former name for the Strait of Gibraltar was the Pillars of Hercules.
3. Atlantis was able to enslave other countries by using its advanced knowledge.
4. The two things that destroyed Atlantis were war with Athens and floods.
5. People want to find Atlantis to better understand it, discover riches and find out if the old stories are true.

Reading strategy: Dictionary skills

Use this reading strategy as a starting point for what you and your students know about the specific skill or language concern. Ask students what they already know about the topic and, after going through the explanation and examples, add your own background information to expand on the ideas. Topics you might want to discuss are:

- Advantages of different kinds of dictionaries, such as English-English and bilingual dictionaries. Students find the latter easier for quickly checking a meaning, but the former helps to build whole language skills and vocabulary.
- Comprehensive dictionaries for home use versus smaller, less comprehensive portable dictionaries.
- Looking for the correct meaning of a word; several meanings are usually listed.

Check student comprehension of the tips that follow by asking students for explanations and examples.

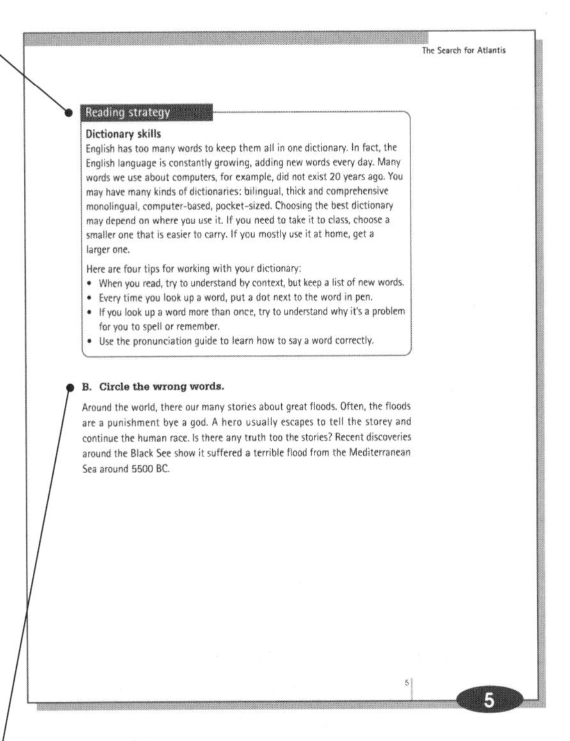

The Search for Atlantis

Reading strategy

Dictionary skills

English has too many words to keep them all in one dictionary. In fact, the English language is constantly growing, adding new words every day. Many words we use about computers, for example, did not exist 20 years ago. You may have many kinds of dictionaries: bilingual, thick and comprehensive monolingual, computer-based, pocket-sized. Choosing the best dictionary may depend on where you use it. If you need to take it to class, choose a smaller one that is easier to carry. If you mostly use it at home, get a larger one.

Here are four tips for working with your dictionary:

- When you read, try to understand by context, but keep a list of new words.
- Every time you look up a word, put a dot next to the word in pen.
- If you look up a word more than once, try to understand why it's a problem for you to spell or remember.
- Use the pronunciation guide to learn how to say a word correctly.

B. Circle the wrong words.

Around the world, there our many stories about great floods. Often, the floods are a punishment bye a god. A hero usually escapes to tell the storey and continue the human race. Is there any truth too the stories? Recent discoveries around the Black See show it suffered a terrible flood from the Mediterranean Sea around 5500 BC.

5

B. Circle the wrong words.

Students should read the paragraph and circle the words used incorrectly. Remind students to check they are choosing the right word when they write, not a homonym.

Answers

Around the world, there **our** (are) many stories about great floods. Often, the floods are a punishment **bye** (by) a god. A hero usually escapes to tell the **storey** (story) and continue the human race. Is there any truth **too** (to) the stories? Recent discoveries around the Black **See** (Sea) show it suffered a terrible flood from the Mediterranean Sea around 5500 BC.

Teaching note

To save yourself time, try different forms of peer editing. For example, after students have finished an exercise, put them in pairs to see if they agree on the answers. As they check each other's work, encourage them to give each other explanations in English for any corrections they might need. In time, you can adapt this technique to longer and more complicated tasks.

Teaching note

Make students responsible for what they study. As they finish each task and unit, remind them that they should understand the ideas completely. If not, it's their responsibility to reread, review and retry the tasks. A useful benchmark is the skills check on page 142 of the Student Book.

C. Fill in the missing words.

Review the vocabulary notes, making sure students can use the words in sentences and new contexts. As an easy task at the end of class, give a comprehension test by giving students the definitions and asking them to supply the words.

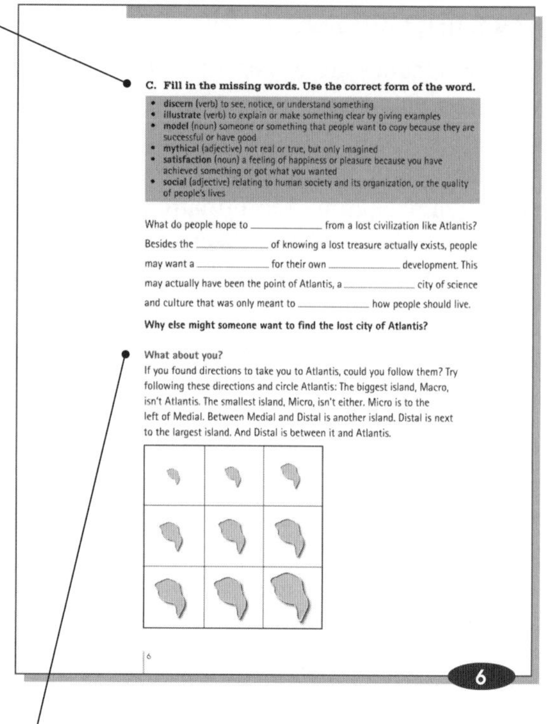

C. Fill in the missing words. Use the correct form of the word.

- **discern** (verb) to see, notice, or understand something
- **illustrate** (verb) to explain or make something clear by giving examples
- **model** (noun) someone or something that people want to copy because they are successful or have good
- **mythical** (adjective) not real or true, but only imagined
- **satisfaction** (noun) a feeling of happiness or pleasure because you have achieved something or got what you wanted
- **social** (adjective) relating to human society and its organization, or the quality of people's lives

What do people hope to ______ from a lost civilization like Atlantis? Besides the ______ of knowing a lost treasure actually exists, people may want a ______ for their own ______ development. This may actually have been the point of Atlantis, a ______ city of science and culture that was only meant to ______ how people should live.

Why else might someone want to find the lost city of Atlantis?

What about you?

If you found directions to take you to Atlantis, could you follow them? Try following these directions and circle Atlantis: The biggest island, Macro, isn't Atlantis. The smallest island, Micro, isn't either. Micro is to the left of Medial. Between Medial and Distal is another island. Distal is next to the largest island. And Distal is between it and Atlantis.

6

Answers

What do people hope to **discern** from a lost civilization like Atlantis? Besides the **satisfaction** of knowing a lost treasure actually exists, people may want a **model** for their own **social** development. This may actually have been the point of Atlantis, a **mythical** city of science and culture that was only meant to **illustrate** how people should live.

Why else might someone want to find the lost city of Atlantis?

Answers

Answers will vary, but two examples are:

- Someone might want the pure adventure of finding a lost city.
- Someone might want the satisfaction of making a great discovery.

Once students have finished the task, discuss the paragraph and how it relates to the main reading.

What about you?

Students should reflect on the question and do the activity suggested.

Encourage students to explain how they found the answer and to draw similar maps of their own with sequential directions.

Answer

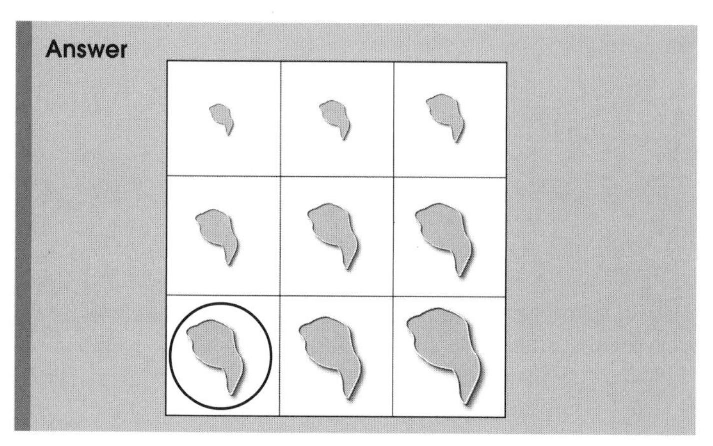

Teaching note

When students enjoy a particular activity, such as the logic problem on this page, direct them to further examples, such as a book on mazes in the library. Each reading should be a starting point for students to learn more about a topic.

Lesson Two

Read about it

Students can listen first, reflecting on the two discussion questions and trying to get the main idea of the passage before they open their books to read. Use the audio recording as often as necessary to help students with pronunciation and general comprehension.

Answers

- Different ways of discussing dates include *era, BC* and *ages.*
- The author does not seem to believe in Atlantis.

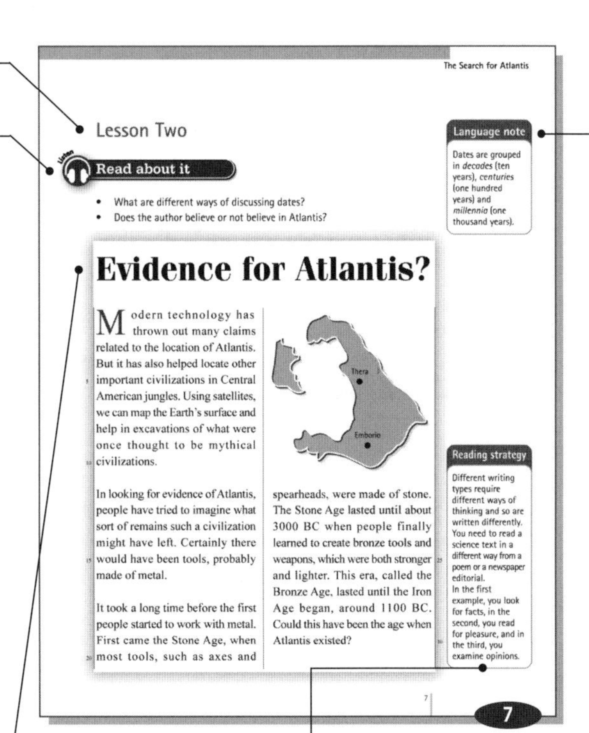

The Search for Atlantis

Lesson Two

Read about it

- What are different ways of discussing dates?
- Does the author believe or not believe in Atlantis?

Evidence for Atlantis?

Modern technology has thrown out many claims related to the location of Atlantis. But it has also helped locate other important civilizations in Central American jungles. Using satellites, we can map the Earth's surface and help in excavations of what were once thought to be mythical civilizations.

In looking for evidence of Atlantis, people have tried to imagine what sort of remains such a civilization might have left. Certainly there would have been tools, probably made of metal.

It took a long time before the first people started to work with metal. First came the Stone Age, when most tools, such as axes and spearheads, were made of stone. The Stone Age lasted until about 3000 BC when people finally learned to create bronze tools and weapons, which were both stronger and lighter. This era, called the Bronze Age, lasted until the Iron Age began, around 1100 BC. Could this have been the age when Atlantis existed?

Language note

Dates are grouped in *decades* (ten years), *centuries* (one hundred years) and *millennia* (one thousand years).

Reading strategy

Different writing types require different ways of thinking and so are written differently. You need to read a science text in a different way from a poem or a newspaper editorial. In the first example, you look for facts, in the second, you read for pleasure, and in the third, you examine opinions.

7

Note: Because of differences in Greek and English alphabets, *Thera* is spelled several ways, such as *Fiera, Thiera, Fera* and *Thara.*

The first paragraph talks about modern technology helping to look for lost cities. The second paragraph discusses general criteria for a search for Atlantis. The third paragraph discusses different materials for tools and relates them to different ages.

Evidence for Atlantis?

This reading gives a scientific perspective to the search for Atlantis and identifies what might be looked for in a search for Atlantis, including evidence of Iron Age tools.

Language note

Review the language note, making sure students understand the general idea.

Reading strategy

Review the reading strategy, making sure students understand the general idea.

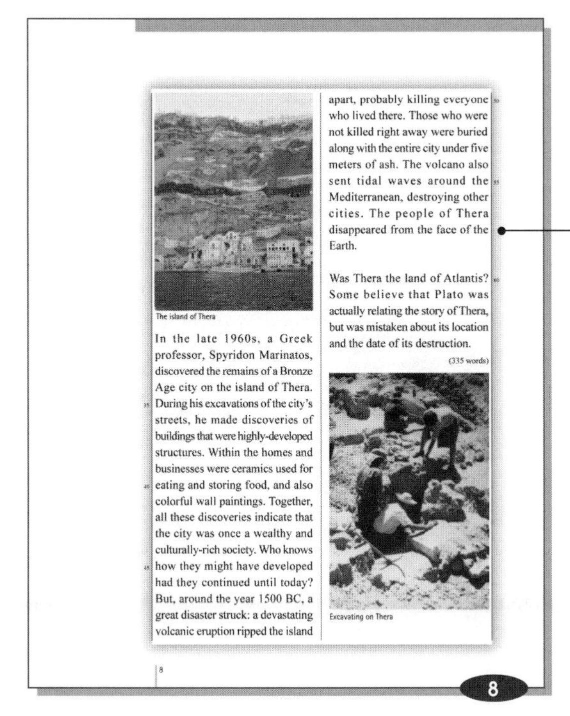

The island of Thera

In the late 1960s, a Greek professor, Spyridon Marinatos, discovered the remains of a Bronze Age city on the island of Thera. During his excavations of the city's streets, he made discoveries of buildings that were highly-developed structures. Within the homes and businesses were ceramics used for eating and storing food, and also colorful wall paintings. Together, all these discoveries indicate that the city was once a wealthy and culturally-rich society. Who knows how they might have developed had they continued until today? But, around the year 1500 BC, a great disaster struck: a devastating volcanic eruption ripped the island apart, probably killing everyone who lived there. Those who were not killed right away were buried along with the entire city under five meters of ash. The volcano also sent tidal waves around the Mediterranean, destroying other cities. The people of Thera disappeared from the face of the Earth.

Was Thera the land of Atlantis? Some believe that Plato was actually relating the story of Thera, but was mistaken about its location and the date of its destruction.

(335 words)

Excavating on Thera

8

The fourth paragraph gives a theory about Atlantis based on the destruction of an ancient city by a volcano. The fifth paragraph raises the question of whether or not this place, Thera, might have been Atlantis.

Teaching note

Get an idea of who are the faster and slower readers by watching them as they read through the articles on their own. For the slower readers, you might privately suggest to them that they try reading ahead of each day's lesson. Also, emphasize that they need to pay particular attention to the reading strategies.

Vocabulary notes

Review the vocabulary notes, making sure students can use the words in sentences and new contexts. An easy task at the end of class is to give a test asking students to write definitions for the words.

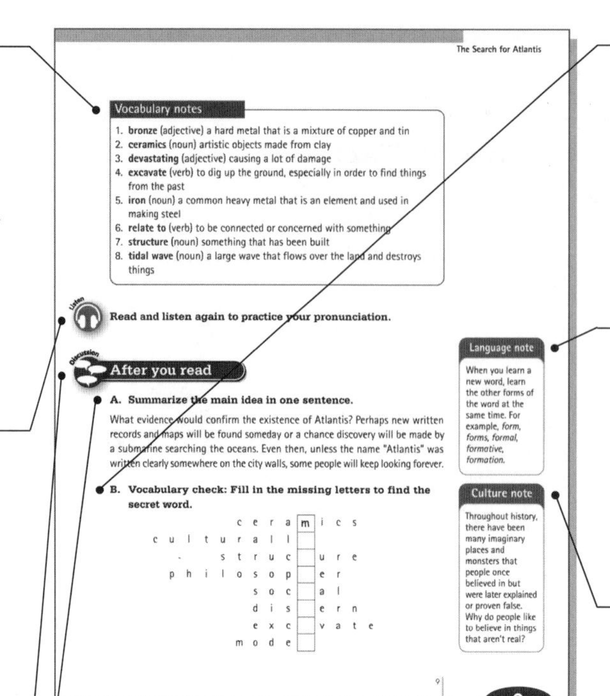

The Search for Atlantis

Vocabulary notes

1. **bronze** (adjective) a hard metal that is a mixture of copper and tin
2. **ceramics** (noun) artistic objects made from clay
3. **devastating** (adjective) causing a lot of damage
4. **excavate** (verb) to dig up the ground, especially in order to find things from the past
5. **iron** (noun) a common heavy metal that is an element and used in making steel
6. **relate to** (verb) to be connected or concerned with something
7. **structure** (noun) something that has been built
8. **tidal wave** (noun) a large wave that flows over the land and destroys things

Read and listen again to practice your pronunciation.

After you read

A. Summarize the main idea in one sentence.

What evidence would confirm the existence of Atlantis? Perhaps new written records and maps will be found someday or a chance discovery will be made by a submarine searching the oceans. Even then, unless the name "Atlantis" was written clearly somewhere on the city walls, some people will keep looking forever.

B. Vocabulary check: Fill in the missing letters to find the secret word.

c e r a [m] i c s
c u l t u r a l l [ ]
s t r u c [ ] u r e
p h i l o s o p [ ] e r
s o c [ ] a l
d i s [ ] e r n
e x c [ ] v a t e
m o d e [ ]

Language note

When you learn a new word, learn the other forms of the word at the same time. For example, *form, forms, formal, formative, formation.*

Culture note

Throughout history, there have been many imaginary places and monsters that people once believed in but were later explained or proven false. Why do people like to believe in things that aren't real?

9

B. Vocabulary check.

Students should fill in the missing letters to find the secret word.

Answer
mythical

Language note

Review the language note, making sure students understand the general idea. Ask students for examples, where appropriate.

Culture note

Review the culture note, making sure students understand the general idea. Add any examples from your own experience.

Read and listen again

This gives students another opportunity to connect the written text to how it is pronounced at both the word and sentence level.

After you read

A. Summarize the main idea in one sentence.

Students should read the paragraph and write one sentence to summarize the main idea.

Answer
Answers will vary, but one example is: It is unlikely that evidence will be found identifying Atlantis that will satisfy everyone.

C. Choose the best answer.

This is a multiple choice exercise to assess students' comprehension of the two readings in the unit.

Answers
1. c, 2. d, 3. b, 4. a, 5. c, 6. d, 7. b, 8. a

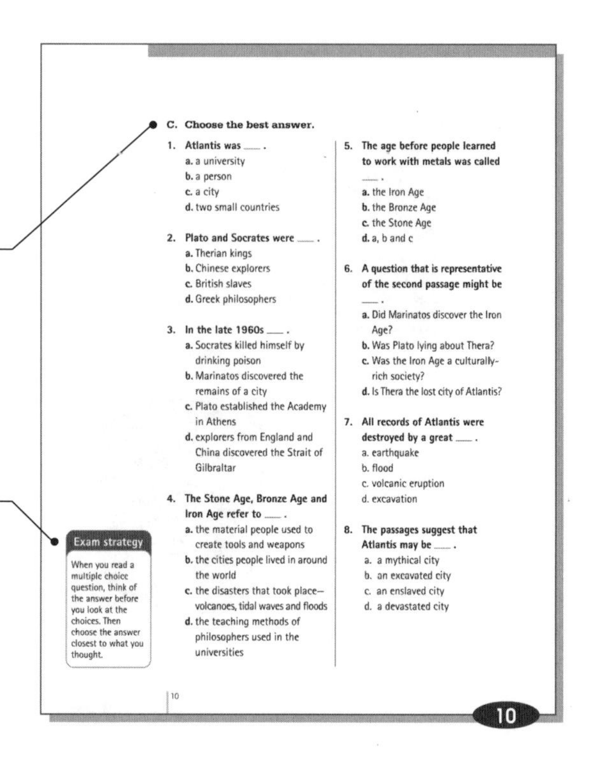

C. Choose the best answer.

1. **Atlantis was ____ .**
   a. a university
   b. a person
   c. a city
   d. two small countries
2. **Plato and Socrates were ____ .**
   a. Therian kings
   b. Chinese explorers
   c. British slaves
   d. Greek philosophers
3. **In the late 1960s ____ .**
   a. Socrates killed himself by drinking poison
   b. Marinatos discovered the remains of a city
   c. Plato established the Academy in Athens
   d. explorers from England and China discovered the Strait of Gilbraltar
4. **The Stone Age, Bronze Age and Iron Age refer to ____ .**
   a. the material people used to create tools and weapons
   b. the cities people lived in around the world
   c. the disasters that took place—volcanoes, tidal waves and floods
   d. the teaching methods of philosophers used in the universities
5. **The age before people learned to work with metals was called ____ .**
   a. the Iron Age
   b. the Bronze Age
   c. the Stone Age
   d. a, b and c
6. **A question that is representative of the second passage might be ____ .**
   a. Did Marinatos discover the Iron Age?
   b. Was Plato lying about Thera?
   c. Was the Iron Age a culturally-rich society?
   d. Is Thera the lost city of Atlantis?
7. **All records of Atlantis were destroyed by a great ____ .**
   a. earthquake
   b. flood
   c. volcanic eruption
   d. excavation
8. **The passages suggest that Atlantis may be ____ .**
   a. a mythical city
   b. an excavated city
   c. an enslaved city
   d. a devastated city

Exam strategy

When you read a multiple choice question, think of the answer before you look at the choices. Then choose the answer closest to what you thought.

10

Exam strategy

Review the exam strategy, making sure students understand the general idea. These notes help students make better use of their time before and during exams. They are collected in an easy-reference appendix at the back of the Student Book on page 143.

Debate

Arrange students in pairs or groups and have them choose the *for* or *against* side of the debate. Each point of view is a *thesis*. Students should use the points that are given as a starting point of their debate, adding information and vocabulary from throughout the unit to build their arguments.

Ask students to write notes supporting their arguments. They should also consider what arguments the other side might have. Don't worry too much about perfect pronunciation. Encourage fluency so that students become more comfortable speaking English and listening to one another.

To stage a debate, follow this format:

- Give each side a few minutes to prepare their arguments. This might also be assigned as homework.
- While one side presents its argument, the other side makes notes for the rebuttal.
- After both sides have presented their arguments, it is time for the rebuttals. Students should focus on the points made by the other side and not introduce new points or repeat their first arguments.
- At the end of the debate, you or a group of students can decide which side of the debate is most convincing and best argued.

The debate section can also be used for essay topics or students can follow up a debate by writing about it.

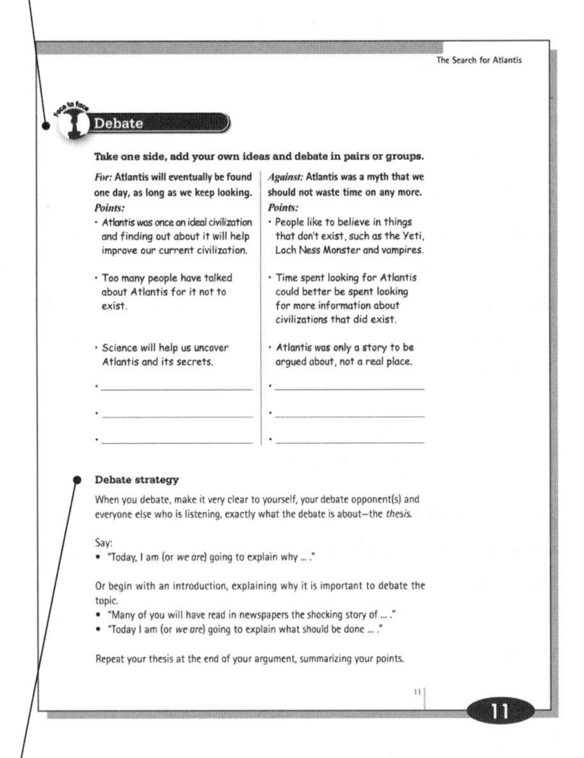
The Search for Atlantis

Face to face

Debate

Take one side, add your own ideas and debate in pairs or groups.

For: Atlantis will eventually be found one day, as long as we keep looking.	*Against:* Atlantis was a myth that we should not waste time on any more.
Points:	*Points:*
• Atlantis was once an ideal civilization and finding out about it will help improve our current civilization.	• People like to believe in things that don't exist, such as the Yeti, Loch Ness Monster and vampires.
• Too many people have talked about Atlantis for it not to exist.	• Time spent looking for Atlantis could better be spent looking for more information about civilizations that did exist.
• Science will help us uncover Atlantis and its secrets.	• Atlantis was only a story to be argued about, not a real place.
• ____________	• ____________
• ____________	• ____________
• ____________	• ____________

Debate strategy

When you debate, make it very clear to yourself, your debate opponent(s) and everyone else who is listening, exactly what the debate is about—the *thesis*.

Say:

- "Today, I am (or *we are*) going to explain why ... ."

Or begin with an introduction, explaining why it is important to debate the topic.

- "Many of you will have read in newspapers the shocking story of ... ."
- "Today I am (or *we are*) going to explain what should be done ... ."

Repeat your thesis at the end of your argument, summarizing your points.

11

11

Debate strategy

Use the debate strategy to teach students ways to get their points of view across to others. Stress that the notes are useful in real life, not just for classroom discussions. In this first strategy, for example, point out that many arguments are lost because people do not agree on the thesis—what they are actually arguing about. For example, a teenager arguing with a parent about how late he or she can stay out may be arguing about many different things, not just the time:

- How safe is it?
- Is the teenager responsible?
- Will the teenager get in trouble?
- Are the teenager's friends irresponsible?
- Does the teenager have obligations the next day?

If a parent simply says, "I don't want you to go" and the teenager says " I want to go", both have a weak thesis and there is no room for debate.

Ask students for other examples.

Don't worry too much if the first debate is not a great success. It might take students a bit of time to build confidence and become more comfortable with the debate format. Persist, and you and your students will see positive results.

The debate strategies are collected in an easy-reference appendix at the back of the Student Book on pages 144–145.

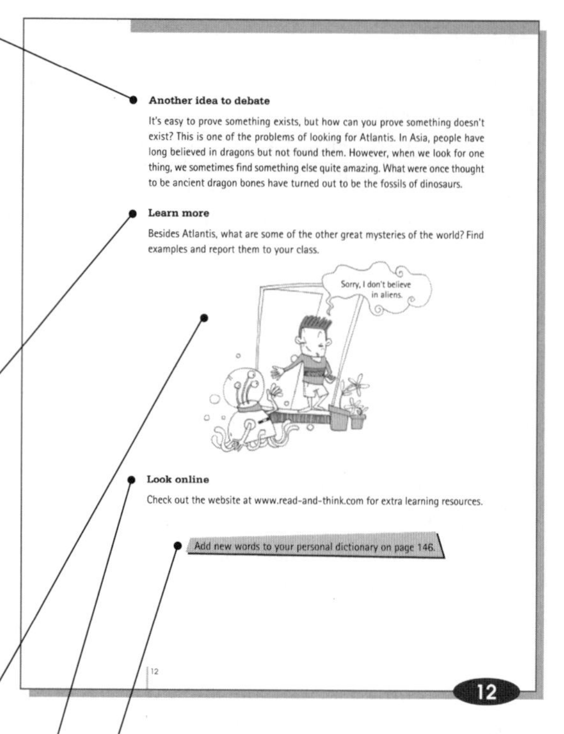

Another idea to debate

It's easy to prove something exists, but how can you prove something doesn't exist? This is one of the problems of looking for Atlantis. In Asia, people have long believed in dragons but not found them. However, when we look for one thing, we sometimes find something else quite amazing. What were once thought to be ancient dragon bones have turned out to be the fossils of dinosaurs.

Learn more

Besides Atlantis, what are some of the other great mysteries of the world? Find examples and report them to your class.

Look online

Check out the website at www.read-and-think.com for extra learning resources.

Add new words to your personal dictionary on page 146.

12

Another idea to debate

This can be used as additional information for one or both sides of the debate or as a starting point for a new topic to debate. Some units feature several quotes that students may need to think about to understand. Students should think about the quotes that are in favor of their thesis. They should also think about how the quotes could be rephrased or adapted to explain a point of view.

Learn more

Follow up this activity with written or oral presentations. Other mysteries include the construction of the giant heads on Easter Island, the spread of early peoples around the world and the stories behind mythical monsters such as Bigfoot, the Abominable Snowman and the Loch Ness Monster.

Review the cartoon

Ask students to explain what they find funny about the cartoon. Ask how the cartoon relates to the content of the unit. In this case, the cartoon suggests that some people don't believe in something even if they have evidence in front of them.

Look online

Encourage students to check out the website at www.read-and-think.com for extra learning resources.

Add new words

Finally, encourage students to add new words to their personal dictionaries in the Student Book on page 146.

Teaching note

If students have access to the WWW, they can use the resources at www.read-and-think.com, but they can also research any topic that interests them. Turn students' questions in class to mini-assignments, asking students to find out a bit more and report back to the class.

Unit 2

The Olympic Games

Fields of study: Tourism, Leisure, Sports

- Tourism is the business of providing information to people about a place they are vacationing in, such as activities to do, places to stay at or facts about the local history or culture. Tourism is now the world's biggest business!
- Leisure is time when you are not working or studying and can relax and do things you enjoy. Those who study leisure look at how people spend their time relaxing.
- Sports are physical activities in which people compete against each other. Those who study sports look at their history and their impact on people individually and in groups.

Lesson One

Background information

This unit examines both good and bad aspects of the Olympic Games, beginning with its origins in ancient Greece. The modern Olympics are an interesting example of the determination of one man, Pierre de Coubertin, to revive an ancient tradition and make it into a new and internationally popular phenomenon. On the other hand, intense competition has also led to extraordinary methods of cheating to win.

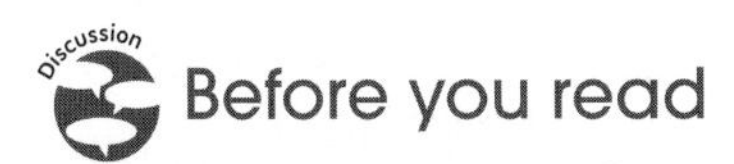

Answers

- The modern Olympic Games were started by Pierre de Coubertin.
- The ancient Olympic Games were first held in 776 BC.

What's happening in this photo?

In 1984, at the XXIII Olympiad (23rd Olympic Games), American Mary Decker became entangled with her chief competitor, South African Zola Budd (front center), and tripped and fell during a race. Another woman won the race.

Ask students how they would feel if they were to watch this happen, as well as what they think the person who fell might have been thinking.

Language note

Answer

XXIX = 29.

Answers

- The sports mentioned include foot and chariot races, discus, boxing, wrestling, fencing, horse riding, rowing, golf, tennis, sailing, shot put, swimming and weightlifting.
- Pierre de Coubertin was a great French athlete who revived the Olympic Games.

The Birth of the Modern Olympics

The icons in circles are for nine Olympic sports. Ask students to identify what sport each represents and write the names on the board: boxing, hurdles, wrestling, discus, fencing, golf, sailing, horse riding, tennis.

The first two paragraphs of the article explain the history of the ancient Olympic Games, which started in 776 BC, near Athens, Greece. Ask students to calculate how long ago that was (776 + this year = number of years ago).

The third paragraph talks about how the Christian Roman Emperor Theodosius decided to terminate the ancient Olympic Games in 393 AD because the games honored Greek gods.

The fourth and fifth paragraphs discuss the revival of the Olympic Games by Pierre de Coubertin and the birth of the modern Olympics. The final paragraph describes the first few modern Olympics.

A theme of the article is the differences between the ancient Olympics and the modern Olympics. Ask students to calculate how long ago the modern Olympics began (this year – 1896 = number of years) and how old de Coubertin was when he died (1937 – 1863 = 74).

Discuss each of the sports in the pictures to make sure students are familiar with them. You may want to ask students to bring pictures of different Olympic sports and athletes from magazines to put on the classroom walls. Add English explanations to each one.

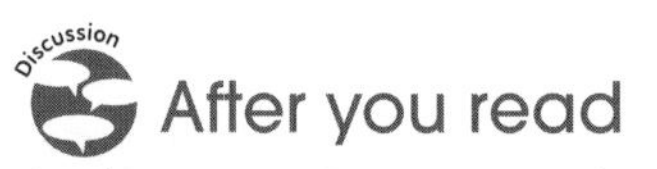

After you read

A. Answer these questions.

Answers

1. The modern Olympics change the events on their program from time to time, but the ancient and modern Olympic Games generally have these sports in common: foot races, boxing and wrestling.
2. The Roman Emperor Theodosius' opposition to the worship of Greek gods led to the end of the ancient Olympics.
3. The phrase *he kept* suggests that the first Olympics also had art and music.
4. Athens, the capital of modern Greece, was the choice of the first modern Olympics because the ancient Olympic Games were held by Greeks near there.
5. de Coubertin might have wanted to restart the Olympic Games because he was interested in promoting athletics and international cooperation.

Reading strategy: Thesaurus skills

A thesaurus is a useful resource for writing and also for learning English. Use this section to make sure that students understand what a thesaurus is and how it is used. Read through the explanation with students. Ask questions to make sure they understand. Explain the four tips and ask students for examples. You may wish to ask students to use a thesaurus to find synonyms and antonyms of some common adjectives such as *big*, *afraid* and *lovely*. Do the synonyms of each word have slightly different meanings?

B. Find synonyms and antonyms in a thesaurus.

Answers

word	synonym	antonym
play (verb)	have fun	work
compete (verb)	race	quit
enjoy (verb)	like	hate
race (noun)	competition	cooperation
lose (verb)	fail	win

C. Fill in the missing words.

Answers

Girls and young women could watch the **ancient** Olympic Games, but married women could not and could be **sentenced** to death if they were caught. Similarly, in the first modern Olympic Games in 1896, women could not compete. In the 1900 Paris Olympics, nineteen women **competed** in three sports: tennis, sailing and golf. The first Gold **medal** in Women's Golfing was won by Margaret Abbot who took the prize because all the French women golfers arrived in **high heels** and tight skirts that weren't **suited** to the game.

What part do women now play in the Olympics?

Answer

Women now compete in nearly every sport which men compete in. Any new sport introduced to the Olympics must be open to male and female competitors.

Lesson Two

Read about it

Answers
- There are many negative points about the Olympics, including unfair competition, drug use and cheating. Not mentioned in the article is that many of the Olympics have been highly political.
- Negative words used to describe unfair practices include *tricks, prohibited, abuse, overdose* and *cheating.*

Olympic Tribulations

Students may not know the word *tribulations*, meaning *problems*. Don't tell them. Rather, let them guess the meaning after reading the passage.

The first paragraph outlines the Olympic Creed. The second paragraph introduces the idea of unfair practices in the Olympics, such as judges voting for political reasons.

The third paragraph talks about athletes who use tricks to cheat and gives an example of illegal equipment use. The fourth paragraph discusses the biggest problem in terms of unfair practices: The use of prohibited drugs.

The fifth paragraph provides an earlier example of cheating from the ancient Olympic Games, where a married woman impersonated a man in order to watch the games.

Ask students to compare this reading with the Lesson One reading. Students should make judgments about the overall worth of the Olympic Games and the motivations of people who cheat at the Olympics.

Teaching note

Bring cartoons to class with blanks in the speech and thought bubbles. It's a fun activity for students to add their own English text.

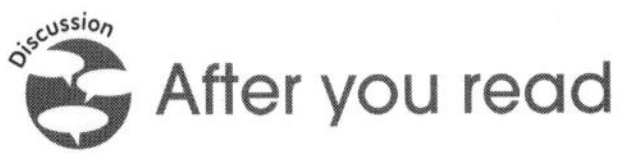

After you read

A. Summarize the main idea in one sentence.

Answer
Answers will vary, but one example is: Although the Japanese may have thought they would win all the Judo events when they introduced the sport to the Olympics, they were surprised that a Dutchman, Anton Geesink, won the open class event.

B. Vocabulary check.

Answers

N	L	Y	F	M	S	T	R	U	G	G	L	E	R	X
A	C	X	A	F	T	L	N	E	Y	M	C	X	O	W
S	H	X	Y	S	A	I	L	I	N	G	F	U	X	K
U	A	J	D	Q	D	E	B	O	X	I	N	G	J	A
W	R	Q	R	P	G	I	H	D	L	I	D	Z	C	F
I	I	V	Q	X	I	R	X	Y	T	R	I	C	K	S
F	O	V	L	P	E	T	H	O	N	O	R	E	D	W
F	T	N	Y	C	O	L	M	P	I	C	S	D	L	R
D	R	A	N	C	I	E	N	T	L	B	J	E	U	E
S	C	O	R	E	N	W	T	X	V	K	U	B	E	S
F	E	N	C	E	D	G	F	A	M	E	D	A	L	T
B	Y	C	O	M	P	E	T	E	D	G	I	C	Y	L
R	O	P	P	O	N	E	N	T	S	N	R	E	A	I
T	O	J	D	I	S	C	U	S	O	C	N	B	T	N
D	V	V	V	M	O	D	E	R	N	V	E	C	C	G

C. Choose the best answer.

Answers
1. c, 2. d, 3. a, 4. a, 5. c, 6. c, 7. d, 8. d

Review the cartoon

The traditional runner is surprised to see the modern runner. In fact, early runners often ran in the nude!

Unit 3
Reach for the Stars

Fields of study: Astronomy, Economics

- Astronomy is the scientific study of the stars and planets, often using telescopes. Astronomy grew out of astrology, which is quite different. Astrology is the study of the positions and movements of the stars and how they might influence people and events.
- Economics is the study of the way in which money and goods are produced and used. Economists collect information to make predictions and recommendations about how governments and businesses should spend and invest.

Lesson One

Background information

This unit looks at the exploration of space from two letters which present different points of view on visits to a science museum. The first letter is more formal and argues that people should support the museum and the country's investment in space. The second letter is informal and presents general impressions of the museum and questions the exhibits.

Before you read

Answers
- The purpose of exploring space is an open-ended question, but answers include finding a new place for people to live, assessing dangers such as asteroids that might hit the Earth and scientific curiosity.
- It's likely that people will eventually live on the Moon and Mars but not too many other planets, at least not in our solar system because they are too inhospitable.

What is happening in this picture?

The picture shows a science fiction illustration of a base on Mars. Ask students if it looks realistic. They should be able to say that it does not, because of the old style of rockets used in comparison to what is used today.

Read about it

Answers
- The different parts of a letter include the sender's address; date; recipient's name, title and address; salutation (*Dear* with the person's name); introduction, body and conclusion; complimentary close; signature; and name under the signature. Other letters have other parts, such as references, subject lines and enclosures.
- This letter is quite formal because the language and tone are formal and it follows a standard format.

A New Home in the Stars

This is a letter to the editor that presents a particular point of view. Ask students about the various parts of the letter and the writer's reason for writing it.

Ask students to explain the different functions of each paragraph of the letter. The first one raises the subject, which is the writer's realization of important issues after seeing two exhibits at a science museum. The second paragraph explains the first exhibit on evolution. The third paragraph talks about the second exhibition, space exploration, and relates it to the second paragraph. In the fourth paragraph, the letter moves into talking about reasons for space exploration. The fifth paragraph gives an action, urging people to visit the museum.

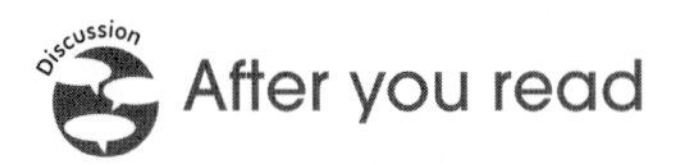

After you read

A. Answer these questions.

Answers
1. The author wants people to support space programs and visit the museum.
2. Two examples the author gives to support her view are Earth's overpopulation problems and satisfying people's natural curiosity.
3. The exhibitions are both temporary, as noted by the word *current*.
4. The author compares exploring space to the first species leaving the seas to move onto land.
5. The author is probably responding to people who suggest that exploring space is a waste of government resources.

Reading strategy: Reading letters

Everyone needs to read and write letters, and understanding their structure is important. Explain this to students and review the explanation and tips with them. As a follow-up activity, you might want to bring—or ask students to bring—letters from home. Sales letters are good choices as they are often both anonymous and quite persuasive. Have students examine the letters and identify the different parts.

B. Write the section each phrase comes from.

Answers
1. salutation
2. action/closing paragraph
3. example
4. date
5. introduction

C. Fill in the missing words.

Answers
Half the **dilemma** of going to Mars is coming back. A **massive** quantity of fuel would be needed for a two-way space voyage. But is it essential? Wouldn't you be willing to become a pioneer on the ultimate **frontier** even if you knew you would never see Earth again? You wouldn't be able to phone home; messages would be delayed ten to twenty-five minutes. But if you planned to make the **noble** choice and stay, the fuel could be **exchanged** for better shelter—and you would need it; the surface of Mars is **buffeted** by 300 kilometer per hour winds and has an average temperature of -63˚C!

What other problems do you think there might be in moving to Mars?

Answer
You would have to improvise a great deal. Everything you want would have to be brought to Mars or made by hand. Although scientists are looking for water on Mars, it might be difficult to find and would be in the form of ice if it were found.

Teaching note

The exploration of space is often in the news and although students may know a lot about space, they probably do not know the names of the common planets, stars and space phenomena in English. Ask each student to "adopt a planet" or some other space phenomena and create a group poster on the wall with all the English vocabulary added.

Lesson Two

Read about it

Answers

- This letter differs from the formal letter in Lesson One in that the language and tone is much more informal. It does not have a return address or the recipient's address. Although it expresses opinions, it does not ask for action. There is no signature before the name typed out.
- The point of view of this letter writer is that the exhibits at the museum are misleading and lacking in key information.

Why Explore the Universe?

This letter takes the opposite point of view of the first letter, and the author does not seem as impressed with the exhibits. This author only wants to share her impressions, not convince the audience.

The letter begins in the first paragraph with criticisms of the evolution exhibit. The reading uses a lot of contractions, such as *didn't* in line 7 and *we'll* in line 10. Ask students if these are more common in formal or informal letters. Explain that contractions are not usually used in formal letters.

The second paragraph introduces the space exhibition, and notes some reservations. These are not expanded upon in the third paragraph which simply summarizes the exhibit. Instead, in the fourth paragraph, the reservations are listed.

The letter ends with a one-sentence paragraph about why the writer thinks scientists prefer space exploration: It's more exciting.

Students should compare the two letters and decide whose opinion they are more likely to follow.

After you read

A. Summarize the main idea in one sentence.

Answer

Answers will vary, but one example is: Space exploration is expensive and the money could instead be used to help people on Earth.

B. Vocabulary check.

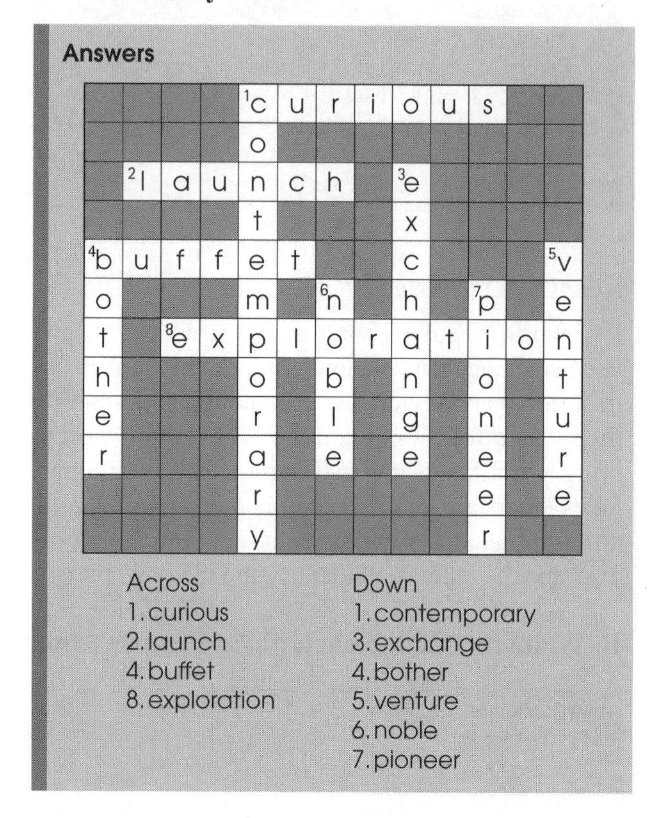

Answers

Across
1. curious
2. launch
4. buffet
8. exploration

Down
1. contemporary
3. exchange
4. bother
5. venture
6. noble
7. pioneer

C. Choose the best answer.

Answers

1. c, 2. c, 3. a, 4. d, 5. d, 6. d, 7. a, 8. c

Review the cartoon

The two spaceships are passing each other, one from the Earth to another planet, the other from another planet to the Earth. The joke is that while we may be trying to escape to another planet, inhabitants on other planets may want to escape to Earth.

Unit 4
The Lord of the Rings

Fields of study: Literature, Biography, Fantasy

- Literature usually refers to books, plays and poems that people think are both important and good. Many novels are written which are interesting for a year or two, but then are forgotten. Literature lasts longer because it conveys important messages rather than simply being entertaining.
- Biography is a book or movie that tells what has happened in someone's life, written by someone else. If you write your own life story, it's called an *autobiography*. Biography is interesting because it helps explain what forces shape a person's life.
- Fantasy refers to an exciting and unusual experience or situation you imagine happening to you, but which will probably never happen. As a genre of literature, it is based on imagination and not facts.

Lesson One

Background information

This unit discusses the life of the author John Ronald Reuel Tolkien and his most famous work, *The Lord of the Rings* trilogy. Tolkien was an interesting person partly because he was not a writer first, but rather a professor of languages. His biography suggests that his stories might have been influenced by his war experiences. Acting out a great fantasy war epic in *The Lord of the Rings* are different characters who represent different parts of society.

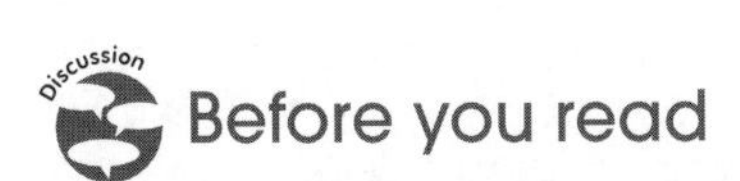

Before you read

Answers
- John Ronald Reuel Tolkien was the author of *The Hobbit* and *The Lord of the Rings* trilogy.
- A metaphor is a figure of speech that compares one thing to another without using *like* or *as*; a simile makes comparisons using *like* or *as*.

Do you recognize anyone in this picture?
The picture is from a movie premiere of *The Lord of the Rings*. The actor Andy Serkis stands behind a model of his character, Gollum.

Read about it

Answers
- The story of *The Lord of the Rings* is about the attempts of a hobbit to destroy an evil ring by returning it to the volcano where it was created.
- *The Lord of the Rings* tells the story of hobbits, wizards, elves and dwarves. Students may know the names of several other groups from having read the story or seen the movie.

Metaphors in *The Lord of the Rings*

This reading tells the story of *The Lord of the Rings* and relates it to an extended metaphor, a struggle between good and evil in which even the smallest can help overcome great evil.

The first paragraph gives the background to the story, explaining how the rings came into being and how one ring got lost. A culture note on page 40 mentions that *The Lord of the Rings* is full of poetry, including one poem which explains the origins of the rings. The full poem from which the couplet is taken is:

Three Rings for the Elven-kings under the sky,
Seven for the Dwarf-lords in their halls of stone,
Nine for the Mortal Men doomed to die,
One for the Dark Lord on his dark throne
In the Land of Mordor where the Shadows lie.
One Ring to rule them all, One Ring to find them,
One Ring to bring them all and in the darkness bind them
In the Land of Mordor where the Shadows lie.

The second paragraph explains how the evil ring passed from one hobbit, Bilbo Baggins to his nephew, Frodo Baggins, who takes on the quest to destroy it.

The fourth paragraph explains that the different groups of characters in *The Lord of the Rings* can be considered to be metaphors for different people in human society.

The picture shows a painting of a shire.

One follow-up question to ask students is which character they would like to be and why.

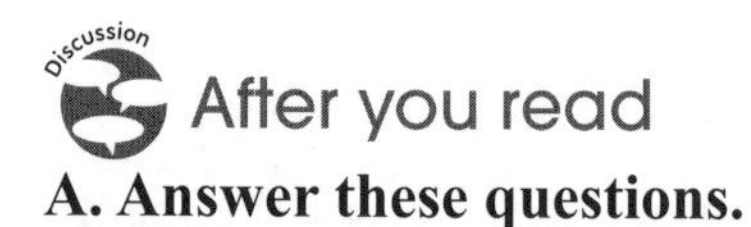

After you read

A. Answer these questions.

> **Answers**
> 1. The main metaphor of *The Lord of the Rings* is the ring, a metaphor for power.
> 2. Tolkien represents different aspects of human nature by giving different groups their own characteristics.
> 3. The author seems to admire elves most and dwarves the least.
> 4. The contrast in the plot of *The Lord of the Rings* is that a small hobbit must be the one to defeat the forces of evil.
> 5. The author sees an ignorance of the rest of the world as a bad side of the simple life.

Reading strategy: Looking at metaphors

Metaphors are important for students to learn about because their meanings are not always apparent from simply reading and understanding individual words. Read through the explanation with students. Ask questions to make sure they understand. Explain the four tips and ask students for examples of metaphors they have read about. Students can also create their own metaphors.

B. Explain the comparisons.

> **Answers**
> 1. To be in hot water means to be in trouble. Spurgeon jokes that he is the one who makes trouble for others.
> 2. Brancusi compares his abilities and fame as a sculptor to Rodin in terms of trees: a small one (himself) and a great one (Rodin). Brancusi feels he won't grow if he is too near Rodin.

C. Match the two parts of the dead metaphors.

> **Answers**
> 1f. body of work
> 2d. foot of a hill
> 3e. head of the class
> 4c. leg of a chair
> 5b. neck of a bottle
> 6a. point in time

Now write definitions for each of the phrases.

> **Answers**
> 1. A large amount of work that has been collected.
> 2. The lowest or bottom part of a hill.
> 3. The top or most important position of the class.
> 4. One of the upright parts that support a chair.
> 5. The narrow part of a bottle, usually near the top.
> 6. An exact moment in time.

Lesson Two

Read about it

> **Answers**
> - A genre is a type of writing that has certain conventions. For example, detective stories have conventions such as surprising twists. This is an example of the genre of biography.
> - Tolkien's childhood could be described as incredibly sad. First his father and then his mother died and when he fell in love with a girl, he was forbidden to continue seeing her.

The Creator of Middle Earth

This short biography tells about the life of J.R.R. Tolkien, author of *The Hobbit* and *The Lord of the Rings* trilogy. The first paragraph tells the story of his life up to the death of his father. The second paragraph talks about his mother's death when he was twelve years old. Note the euphemism *passed away* for *died* in line 19.

The second paragraph also mentions his love for a young woman who later became his wife.

The third paragraph relates how Tolkien's love of languages was used to help him in his university studies.

The fourth paragraph talks about Tolkien's war experiences and the loss of his friends. This paragraph also mentions his major works: *The Hobbit* and *The Lord of the Rings* trilogy.

A general question when one reads biographies of authors is how much of their stories are autobiographical. Ask students, "What in Tolkien's life might have influenced him to write *The Hobbit* and *The Lord of the Rings* trilogy?"

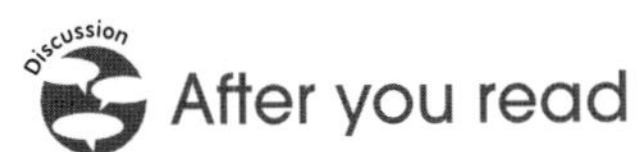

After you read

A. Summarize the main idea in one sentence.

Answer
Answers will vary, but one example is: Peter Jackson used a metaphor to compare his love of New Zealand to a shire and his hatred of Hollywood to Mordor.

B. Vocabulary check.

Answer
metaphor

C. Choose the best answer.

Answers
1. a, 2. c, 3. b, 4. d, 5. a, 6. a, 7. b, 8. b, 9. d, 10. c

Review the cartoon

The cartoon suggests that reading too much on one subject can change the way you look.

Teaching note

Students often have difficulty reading novels and may need guidance. One way to help them is to introduce plot summaries, commonly available on the WWW, sometimes chapter by chapter. When students understand the general plot of a novel, it's easier for them to concentrate on the language they are reading and guess new vocabulary in context.

Unit 5
Small Is Beautiful

Fields of study:
Environment, Economics, Sociology

- Environment studies or environmental studies look at the air, water and land on the Earth, which can be harmed by people's activities. It is concerned with living things and how they live together.
- Economics is the study of the way in which money and goods are produced and used. Economists collect information to make predictions and recommendations about how governments and businesses should spend and invest.
- Sociology is the scientific study of societies and the behavior of people in groups. Sociology is important in many other fields, such as business. For example, sociologists studying business may examine the ways in which people behave differently when in a group compared to how they act when they are alone.

Lesson One

Background information
This unit looks at economics from different perspectives, beginning with the work of an economist, E.F. Schumacher, who challenged some of the basic beliefs about whether people should always try to consume more and whether that should be a measure of success and happiness. The second reading looks at people who take his ideas further, fighting against governments and large companies, but who sometimes have questionable motivations.

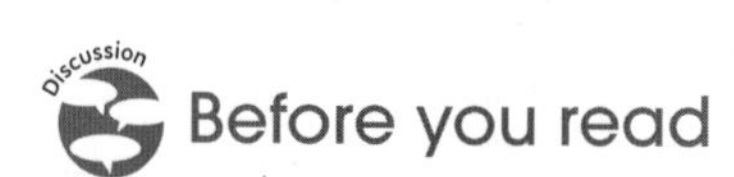

Answers
- Big businesses can help and hurt people in different ways. They help people by providing employment and goods and services. They can hurt people by not paying fairly for the products they use.
- E.F. Schumacher was an economist and author of a book, *Small Is Beautiful: Economics as if People Mattered.*

What's happening in the picture?
Ask students what makes sense to them in the picture. They may recognize that the man's hand is making a peace sign which may also be a victory sign. They may not know the words *corporate* (big companies) and *tyranny* (evil government), or the abbreviation *WTO* (World Trade Organization).

Answers
- Let students listen to hear where there are periods and commas used to signal series, clauses and the ends of sentences. Let them match what they hear to what they read.
- A Buddhist economist is the opposite of a modern economist.

Buddhist Economics

The first paragraph introduces the author of *Small Is Beautiful*, a book which raises questions about the way we make money and what we use it for.

The second paragraph introduces the idea of a Buddhist economist in an extended quote from the book. Note the use of the ellipsis in line 13 that shows a break in the quote where some information has been omitted.

The third paragraph raises other questions about what people really want and what they really need.

The fourth and fifth paragraphs give an example of an extra TV and how it can split a family's time together. It's an example of wealth that might be misspent.

Ask students about the picture of the small dollar. It is a visual metaphor: A shrinking dollar means the dollar is worth less or has decreasing value.

A. Answer these questions.

Answers
1. Two systems of economics, modern and Buddhist, are compared in the reading.
2. Schumacher's point of view on modern economics is that it misses the point of improving life for the sake of creating profit.
3. The title of the book, *Small Is Beautiful*, might mean that instead of thinking big, we should concern ourselves with the small things in life that make us happy.
4. The phrase "standard of living" is in quotation marks to show that the author thinks it is questionable.
5. As above, "better off" is in quotation marks to show that it is questionable.

Reading strategy: Commas and periods

Students will generally be familiar with punctuation in simple and compound sentences, but may still experience problems when faced with its use in complex sentences. Read through the explanation with students. Ask questions to make sure they understand. Explain the four tips and point out examples in the text.

Note: students who have studied British English will know the *period* as a *full stop*.

B. Add the correct punctuation.

Answers
1. The world's forests, mines and oceans won't last forever.
2. While the stock market is important, it's not the only measure of wealth.
3. Poor countries, especially in Africa, can't compete against developed nations.
4. E.F. Schumacher's book, *Small Is Beautiful*, has made people think.
5. Progress, especially in the developed world, should not be paid for by the developing world.

C. Fill in the missing words.

Answers
"The strength of the idea of **private enterprise** lies in its terrifying **simplicity**. It suggests that **totality** of life can be reduced to one **aspect**: profits. The businessman, as a private individual, may still be interested in other aspects of life—perhaps even in goodness, truth, and beauty—but as a businessman he concerns himself only with profits ... private enterprise is not concerned with what it produces but only with what it gains from **production**."
E.F. Schumacher

What else is wrong with companies that just look for profit?

Answer
Answers will vary, but one example is: Such companies ignore the welfare of their workers and exploit people from whom they get their services and resources.

Lesson Two

Answers
- The author's point of view on anti-globalization protests is that the people making the protests are sometimes misguided and don't follow their principles.
- For the purpose of each paragraph, see below.

Anti-Globalization: Problems and Solutions

This reading presents a contrary point of view to the reading in Lesson One.

The first paragraph establishes the discussion, showing what people have to protest about and discusses the people who protest: activists. Paragraph two suggests that these protests are not just battles between heroes and villains.

Paragraphs three and four criticize anti-globalization activists and provide an example of how their principles don't always extend to their personal behavior.

Ask students to explain the last paragraph and relate it to the example, explaining what activists might do to make a better impression.

Ask students about the photograph. Ask what other ways there are to protest; for example, boycotting a good or service.

After you read

A. Summarize the main idea in one sentence.

Answer
Answers will vary, but one example is: You should stand up for others so there will be someone to stand up for you.

B. Vocabulary check.

Answers

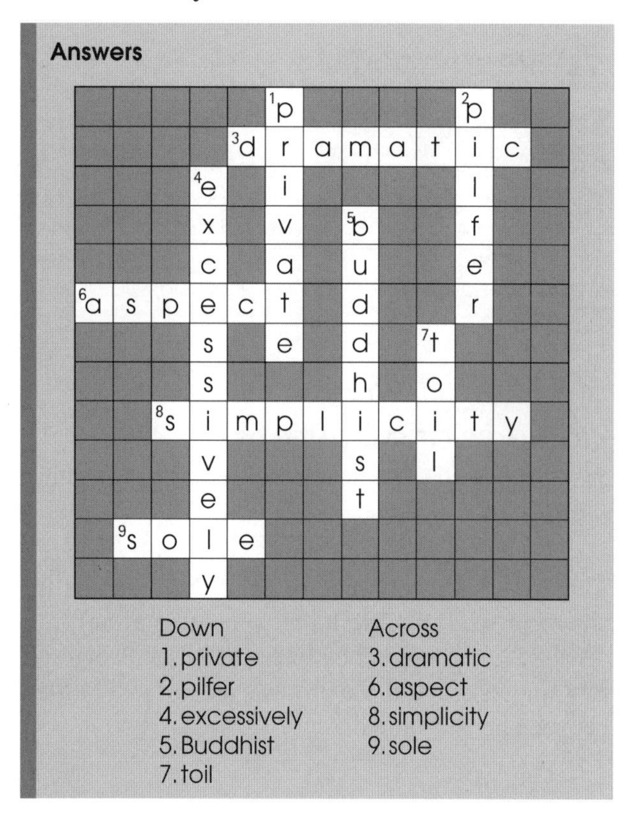

Down
1. private
2. pilfer
4. excessively
5. Buddhist
7. toil

Across
3. dramatic
6. aspect
8. simplicity
9. sole

C. Choose the best answer.

Answers
1. c, 2. b, 3. c, 4. a, 5. c, 6. b, 7. a, 8. b

Review the cartoon

The cartoon shows people protesting offshore oil drilling, but riding a truck running on oil from such a source.

Teaching note

When common affixes, such as the prefix *anti-*, are introduced, draw attention to their importance by asking students what other common words they know that start or end in the same way. Examples for *anti-* include *antibiotic*, *antibody*, *anticlimax*, *antiseptic*, *antisocial* and *antithesis*.

Unit 6

Is Money Everything?

Fields of study:
Philosophy, Psychology, Business

- Philosophy includes the study of the nature and meaning of existence, truth, good and evil. Philosophy often challenges why we do certain things.
- Psychology is the study of the mind and how it influences people's behavior. Psychology is important in many different fields where it is necessary to understand people's actions and reactions.
- Business is the activity of making money by producing or buying and selling goods, or providing services. Business is essential to supplying people with all the things they need—and many that they don't need.

Lesson One

Background information

This unit builds on the preceding one by looking at money from a different, more personal, perspective. The two articles supply a contrast with the first in favor of increased personal wealth and the second article questioning it as the basis of happiness. The first article talks about two billionaires while the second quotes an economist who has identified six factors which lead to happiness.

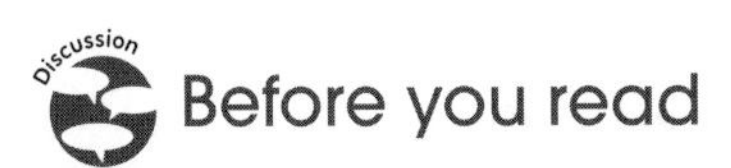

Answer
Answers will vary for the three questions, but ask students to give reasons for their answers.

Check ☑ the diagram to indicate what you understand.

Answer
Student responses will vary. Ask those who understand each point to explain it in their own words.

Label Maslow's level on each picture.

Answers
a. self-actualization
b. safety needs
c. physical needs

Answers
- The title is part of a quote about happiness: "Early to bed early to rise, makes a man healthy, wealthy and wise." The subheadings refer to three aspects of wealth.
- The article is in favor of being wealthy.

Healthy, Wealthy and Wise

The first paragraph is about measuring wealth by how it is spent, not how it is kept.

The second paragraph is about the benefits of wealth to an individual.

The third paragraph talks about how Bill Gates has made others wealthy.

Review the pictures, asking students whether they would like to have a private jet or be Bill Gates. Ask what they would do with their wealth.

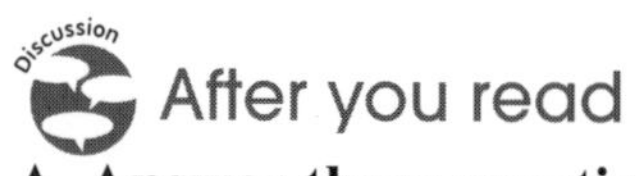

After you read

A. Answer these questions.

Answers
1. Adnan Khashoggi was once one of the world's wealthiest people.
2. The article suggests that the important thing about having money is having more choices.
3. Bill Gates helps make other people wealthy by employing them in his companies, as well as giving ordinary people software tools that help them become more productive.
4. People have always pursued money because it brings freedom to do what they want.
5. The title of the article refers to the ingredients for happiness.

Reading strategy: Survey

Surveying is a common reading strategy to approach the text with a purpose. The easiest way to get students involved in using survey techniques is to question them as they read, stopping before and after titles, paragraphs and sections. Read through the explanation with students. Ask questions to make sure they understand. Explain the four tips and ask students for examples of different text types and how they might approach them.

B. Guess what each title is about.

Answers
Answers will vary, but sample answers include:
1. Ways to manage your money.
2. How money is not the source of happiness.
3. The dangers of gambling.
4. Ways to manage your money by not using credit cards.
5. Why it is best to invest money in education.

C. Fill in the missing words.

Answers
Note: students may change the order of the words in the last quote.

- "Today the greatest single **source** of wealth is between your ears." *Brian Tracy (1944-) Motivational speaker*
- "Early to bed, early to rise, makes a man healthy, wealthy and **wise**." *Benjamin Franklin (1706-1790)*
- "The real **measure** of your wealth is how much you'd be worth if you lost all your money." *Unknown*
- "Being extremely **prosperous** and **virtuous** at the same time is impossible." *Plato (428-348 BC)*

What other sayings about money do you know?

Answer
There are many, but one anonymous example is "A fool and his money are soon parted."

Lesson Two

Read about it

Answers
- Answers will vary, but the best way to measure wealth is in terms of the happiness it brings.
- Answers will vary, but the message of the passage is that money is not as important as the things that it buys.

Money Isn't Everything

This reading provides a contrast to the reading in Lesson One. The theme of the article is that money can bring unhappiness as well as happiness.

The first paragraph questions whether money makes people happier and concludes it does, but only to a certain level after which it often depends on how you compare yourself to others.

The second paragraph uses the example of China's "little emperors," the name for children who are spoiled because they are the only child and grandchild.

The third paragraph gives an economist's view of happiness and suggests time is a better payment. This is similar to the "freedom" mentioned in lines 19 and 20 of the Lesson One reading.

The last paragraph builds on the time idea to talk about how people spend their time.

Using the picture as a starting point, ask students why they might want to volunteer to offer medical or other services in another country.

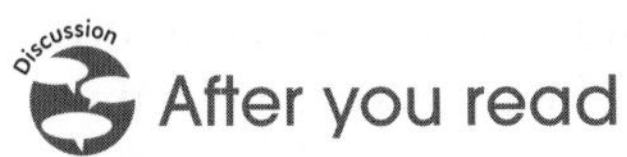

After you read

A. Summarize the main idea in one sentence.

Answer
Answers will vary, but one example is: People's expectations increase with their incomes. Another example is: Telephones are an example of how people always want more than they have.

B. Vocabulary check.

Answers

B	C	O	U	N	T	L	E	S	S	H	E	W	X	E
B	E	W	S	A	S	B	R	E	A	I	E	I	D	T
S	V	I	R	T	U	O	U	S	O	N	S	S	I	A
E	S	D	B	N	S	B	E	T	M	C	E	E	D	M
C	P	U	R	S	U	E	Y	E	E	O	C	Z	L	E
R	P	S	E	M	S	S	S	E	L	M	H	Y	M	T
E	O	H	C	O	S	E	D	M	E	E	E	E	E	O
T	V	F	S	R	W	E	S	C	C	S	E	E	A	E
G	E	F	S	A	F	F	L	U	E	N	T	W	S	B
S	R	R	G	L	S	S	T	U	D	Y	C	I	U	A
B	T	A	E	U	A	E	G	E	E	E	A	S	R	S
J	Y	P	R	O	S	P	E	R	O	U	S	C	E	E
I	D	V	S	S	T	G	E	N	T	P	C	H	W	E
M	P	O	V	E	R	T	Y	Y	P	S	P	U	R	D

C. Choose the best answer.

Answers
1. b, 2. b, 3. b, 4. a, 5. c, 6. b, 7. a, 8. d, 9. a, 10. c

Review the cartoon

The cartoon shows the contrast between the fantasy of a glamorous car in an exotic setting portrayed by an ad and the reality of driving the car on a polluted and boring city street.

Teaching note

As a follow-up idea to puzzles in this and other books, ask students to write sentences using all the words. They should try to fit as many of the words as possible into as few sentences as possible.

Unit 7
What Killed the Dinosaurs?

Fields of study: Paleontology, Geology

- Paleontology is the study of fossils—ancient bones, plants and other things that have been preserved in rock. Paleontology is a kind of detective work which tries to understand life in the distant past.
- Geology is the study of the rocks and soil that make up the Earth, and of the way they have changed since the Earth was formed. Geology is important to mining as well as finding a record of what changes happened on the Earth millions of years ago.

Lesson One

Background information

This unit looks at the mass extinction of the dinosaurs and puts forward several different ideas about what might have happened to them. The main theories in the first reading relate to disease, aliens, egg-eating mammals, parasites, insects and poisonous plants. The second reading's theories involve volcanoes and a meteorite.

Answers
- The last dinosaurs lived 65 million years ago.
- There are many theories of how the last dinosaurs died: mammals eating their eggs, parasites, insects, poisonous plants, a meteorite hitting the earth and volcanic eruptions. There are also some less-likely theories, such as all dinosaurs caught the same disease or they were eaten by aliens.

What's happening in this picture?

The picture shows a girl who appears to be being eaten by a dinosaur. However, humans and dinosaurs are separated by 63 million years. This is at a park in London, England.

Answers
- Adverbs and adjectives describe actions and things respectively.
- Mary Anning was the first to excavate a complete dinosaur skeleton. She did so when still a teenager.

Where Did They Go?

This reading talks about how dinosaur bones were discovered, how dinosaurs were named and the different theories of how dinosaurs became extinct.

In the first paragraph, interpretations of dinosaur bones were difficult because people did not understand what they might be as no complete skeleton was found.

The second paragraph talks about Mary Anning, who excavated the first complete dinosaur skeleton when she was twelve years old and helped the man who gave dinosaurs their name.

The third and fourth paragraphs talk about the extinction of dinosaurs, but end with a puzzle to the various extinction theories.

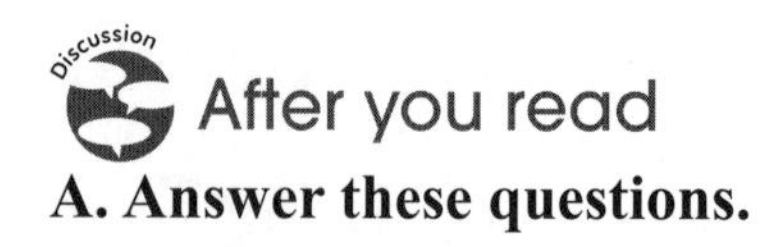

A. Answer these questions.

Answers
1. Different ways dinosaurs might have become extinct include a disease, alien abduction, mammals eating their eggs, parasites, insects and poisonous plants.
2. People and dinosaurs are separated by 63 million years.
3. Carnivorous dinosaurs mostly ate meat—especially other dinosaurs.

4. Lice and flies could have driven a dinosaur mad.
5. Answers will vary, but the idea of aliens eating dinosaurs is a bizarre theory because they would probably have left traces.

Reading strategy: Adjectives and adverbs

Adjectives and adverbs are two important parts of speech that students should be familiar with. Read through the explanation with students. Ask questions to make sure they understand. Explain the four tips and ask students for examples of adverbs and adjectives from the readings.

B. Underline the adjectives and circle the adverbs.

Answers
1. The largest dinosaurs **only** ate vegetation.
2. Dinosaurs could have been green or pink; fossils don't show colors.
3. People searching **hard** for dinosaurs should look at their modern relatives: chickens.
4. Dinosaurs **gradually** evolved over millions of years into giant creatures.
5. The last dinosaurs **quickly** died **together** around the same time.

What else do you know about dinosaurs and dinosaur fossils?

Answer
Answers will vary, but encourage students to discuss and share their ideas.

C. Fill in the missing words.

Answers
China is a country popular with dinosaur hunters. The first **record** of a dinosaur bone was made around 300 BC, by a Chinese **scholar** named Chang Qu, who lived in Wucheng, Sichuan. Chang found a dinosaur **fossil**. He could only **imagine** it was a dragon bone. It wasn't until the 1850s, more than two thousand years later, that people began to **comprehend** the great age of dinosaurs.

Lesson Two

Answers
- The two main theories in this article are about dinosaurs being killed by volcanic eruptions or a meteorite hitting the Earth.
- The consequences of each disaster include the air filling with dust and becoming difficult to breathe, the Earth becoming colder as the sun is blocked out, difficulty in growing food crops due to lack of sunlight and ash covering the ground, production of gasses that choke people, and the formation of tidal waves and forest fires.

An Explosive End?

This article explores two more likely reasons for the extinction of dinosaurs.

The first paragraph explains the search for a theory that explains the death of the dinosaurs.

The next three paragraphs focus on the volcano theory of the destruction of the dinosaurs, describing what happened when the most explosive volcano in recent history erupted in 1815.

The final paragraph introduces the meteorite theory, but still leaves room for doubt.

The reading presents opportunities for students to give their opinions of the best argument for what killed the dinosaurs.

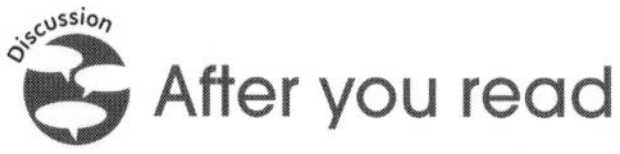

After you read

A. Summarize the main idea in one sentence.

Answer
Answers will vary, but one example is: Two scientists discovered a layer of dust that suggests a large meteorite struck the Earth around the time of the death of the dinosaurs.

B. Vocabulary check.

Answer
meteorite

C. Choose the best answer.

Answers
1. d, 2. d, 3. b, 4. c, 5. b, 6. a, 7.a 8. d

Review the cartoon

The word *thesaurus* sounds like a kind of dinosaur rather than a book of synonyms and antonyms.

Teaching note

Dinosaur names are good for practicing pronunciation because they are generally long and feature multiple syllables. Moreover, many students know the names of certain dinosaurs because of their popularity in books and movies. Help students practice their pronunciation by placing pictures of the dinosaurs on the wall. Have students label the pictures in English. After a while, you can cover the labels to see how well students remember the names. Adapt this technique to any key vocabulary you want students to practice.

Teaching note

In every class, there are more able and less able students. Encourage them to help each other by arranging them in pairs. An important goal in teaching is to make sure that students are neither bored nor frustrated. Giving more able students a chance to help others is a good way to keep them happy and reinforce what they have learned.

Unit 8
Looking for Lost Treasure!

Fields of study:
Cartography, Archaeology, History

- Cartography is the activity of making maps and a cartographer also studies maps to try to understand the thinking of people who devised them.
- Archaeology is the study of ancient societies by examining what remains of their buildings, graves, tools and other artifacts. Archaeologists help explain the daily lives of people who have died long ago.
- History is the study of past events, especially the political, social or economic development of a nation. History is always changing as new facts are found and old facts are reinterpreted.

Lesson One

Background information

This unit focuses on five treasures, four in the first reading and one in the second. Part of the focus of this unit is the human element in finding lost treasure. The first reading focuses on greed while the second one is more concerned with curiosity and risk.

Answers
- You're most likely to find lost treasure where ancient peoples have lived or traveled.
- People lose treasure through accidents, forgetfulness and wars.

What is happening in the picture?

This picture shows the modern discovery of a lost treasure. An underwater scuba diver works at a wreck of a ship, recovering ancient ceramics.

Answer
- Listen for the different ways treasure has been found (digging in a field, looking for a lost goat, digging a well, diving for a lost basket).

Lucky Accidents

The theme of this article is treasure found by accident and is set chronologically into four separate narratives.

Paragraph one is about a farmer who finds Roman silver.

Paragraph two is about the discovery of the Dead Sea Scrolls by young boys looking for a lost goat.

Paragraph three is about the discovery of the terracotta soldiers in Xian, China by farmers digging a well.

Paragraph four tells the story of the discovery of a Chinese trading ship in the Philippines.

The fifth and final paragraph adds a twist to the article, explaining how the first of the four discoverers was cheated out of his find.

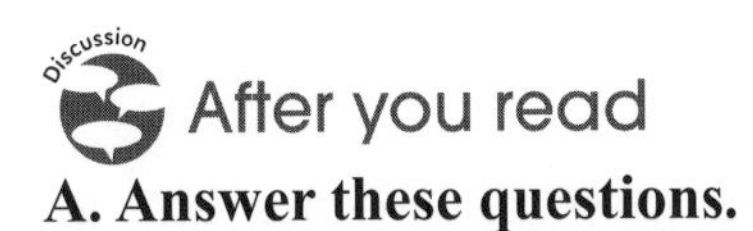

A. Answer these questions.

Answers
1. Among the treasures discovered by accident were Roman silver, the Dead Sea Scrolls, the terracotta soldiers and a Chinese trading junk.
2. Ford might have cheated Butcher for both fame and money.
3. The boys found the manuscripts while searching for a lost goat.
4. The expression *found their way* in this case means they were sold from person to person.
5. Each of the different discoveries are valuable because they add to our understanding of history.

Reading strategy: Phrasal verbs

Phrasal verbs are difficult for students because they must be memorized and do not always follow logical rules. Read through the explanation with students. Ask questions to make sure they understand. Explain the four tips and ask students for examples. Encourage students to collect examples of phrasal verbs.

B. Add words such as *in*, *over*, *out* and *on* to make phrasal verbs and write the definition for each one.

Answer
There are many possible answers. Ask students to explain their choices and check the meanings by asking them to use the words in sentences.

C. Number these sentences in order.

Answers
3, 6, 7, 1, 5, 2, 4

D. Fill in the missing words.

Not all treasure is found **accidentally**. In England, old coins are often found in places where there was once a **settlement**. Fifteen-year-old John Philpotts had been looking for buried treasure since 1992. In 1996, he made a **rare** and important discovery. Using a **metal detector**, he was searching a farmer's field when a **signal** told him there was metal below. John found U.S.$100,000 worth of Roman coins.

Would you like to hunt for buried treasure? Why or why not?

Answer
Answers will vary, but students should give reasons for their answers.

Lesson Two

Read about it

Answers

- The mystery of Oak Island is whether or not treasure is actually buried there.
- People have been searching Oak Island since 1795.

The Mystery of Oak Island

This article tells the history of the discovery of a pit on Oak Island, Canada and its exploration over the course of about two hundred years.

The article features a timeline, with a sentence or two summarizing what happened in each of the key years.

It's not clear why someone built the elaborate traps and pit and whether or not there is actually treasure at the bottom. The mystery may never be solved.

Discussion

After you read

A. Summarize the main idea in one sentence.

Answer
Answers will vary, but one example is: Dr. Robert Ballard discovered the wreck of the *Titanic*, but decided not to raise it as it was also a mass grave.

B. Vocabulary check.

Answer
parchment

C. Choose the best answer.

Answers
1. c, 2. b, 3. a, 4. d, 5. a, 6. c, 7. d, 8. a

More ideas to debate

Answer
Forty feet below two million pounds are buried.

Review the cartoon

The boy and girl each see the same thing but value it differently. A popular expression for this is "Beauty is in the eye of the beholder," which means that people's ideas of beauty are quite individual.

Unit 9
Into Battle!

Fields of study: Military studies, History

- Military studies look at history related to an army, navy or air force. A focus in military studies is how battles are won or lost, based on innovative tactics or unusual conditions.
- History is the study of past events, especially the political, social or economic development of a nation. History is always changing as new facts are found and old facts are reinterpreted.

Lesson One

Background information

This unit examines a famous battle, the Battle of Agincourt, from two perspectives. The first reading gives the background to the battle and the second reading focuses on playwright William Shakespeare's description of it along with a speech by King Henry V that has made the battle extremely famous. Together, the two readings help to show the difference between history and literature.

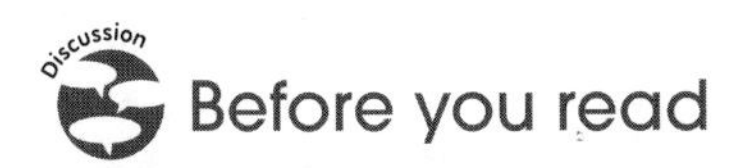

Answers
- The Battle of Agincourt was a fight between the forces of the English and French kings.
- The battle took place on October 25, 1415, between King Henry V of England and Charles VI of France. King Henry V won.

What weapons are the soldiers using to fight?

The soldiers are using spears, axes and swords, and defending themselves with shields.

Answers
- The battle was fought using longbows, crossbows, swords, axes and spears.
- Conjunctions are words used to join phrases.

The Battle of Agincourt

This article tells the story of the Battle of Agincourt, a decisive battle between the French and the English in 1415. The battle is famous for two things: a speech given before it by the English king, Henry V, and his great victory over the French who had 30,000 soldiers to his 10,000.

The first paragraph gives a general background to the battle and is followed in paragraph two with information about the battle and Henry V's speech, the subject of the reading in Lesson Two.

The third paragraph talks about the challenge of the battle and how it ends with a surprising weapon that benefited the English: mud.

The fourth paragraph explains how the mud helped the English win the battle after the French were provoked into charging and became trapped in the mud by their heavy armor.

Ask students to look at the map of the battle scene and imagine what it looked like in reality.

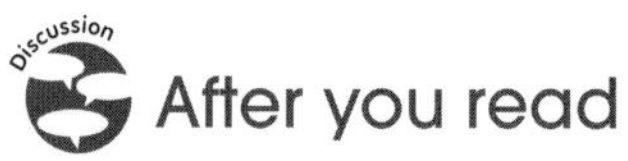

After you read

A. Answer these questions.

Answers

1. The English and French armies were fighting.
2. Territory and the spoils of war might have been two reasons why they fought.
3. The English used strategy to get the French to charge into an unfavorable position.
4. The French soldiers' armor was not an advantage because it weighed them down in the mud.
5. Henry V gave a speech to rally his soldiers and give them courage before the battle to make them fight harder.

Reading strategy: Conjunctions

Conjunctions are vital in English for understanding and expressing complex thoughts. Students tend to overuse simple conjunctions such as *and* and *but*, and ignore others that could help explain deeper meanings. Read through the explanation with students. Ask questions to make sure they understand. Explain the four tips and ask students for examples from the text and other readings they come across.

B. Join the sentences with the conjunctions.

Answers

1. Everyone had to fight or they would be captured.
2. The English nobles weren't worried since they would be ransomed.
3. The other soldiers might be taken as prisoners but they would be killed.
4. Their jewels would be taken and their bodies would be left to rot.
5. King Henry V ordered all French prisoners killed before they could turn on the English.

C. Fill in the missing words.

Answers

As the French began to lose, English soldiers seized prisoners for **ransom** and **scavenged** armor and **jewelry** from the dead. However, the battle was not over and the remaining French still easily outnumbered the English. As French leaders tried to rally their troops for another attack, Henry V gave the order to kill the **prisoners**. This removed the risk of them turning on their **captors** and freed their guards for **combat**.

What other strategies do armies use in battle?

Answer

Answers will vary, but one example is: Armies use many strategies, such as psychological warfare (making the other side afraid) and making their armies seem bigger than they really are.

Lesson Two

Read about it

Answers

- Shakespeare's English is full of different spellings and pronunciations compared with English today. It also contains many words and phrases which are no longer used or used in the same way.
- There are many examples of repetition to add emotion to the speech, such as the repeating of *St. Crispian's day* and *we* in "We few, we happy few, we band of brothers."

Band of Brothers

This passage is about the speech King Henry V gave before the Battle of Agincourt to rally his troops.

The first paragraph explains why Henry V decided to give a speech.

The second paragraph talks about how Henry V's speech was made famous in William Shakespeare's play, *Henry V*.

The third paragraph explains why the speech is difficult to understand because of differences between Shakespeare's English and English today, but students should be able to follow the general meaning and use the notes in the concepts box on page 103 to clarify some of the odd spellings and phrases. The speech then follows.

After the speech, there is an explanation of how Shakespeare's play differs from the actual events.

After you read

A. Summarize the main idea in one sentence.

Answer
Answers will vary, but one example is: The French version of the story was that King Henry V warned his soldiers to fight or be killed; as King, he would simply be ransomed.

B. Vocabulary check.

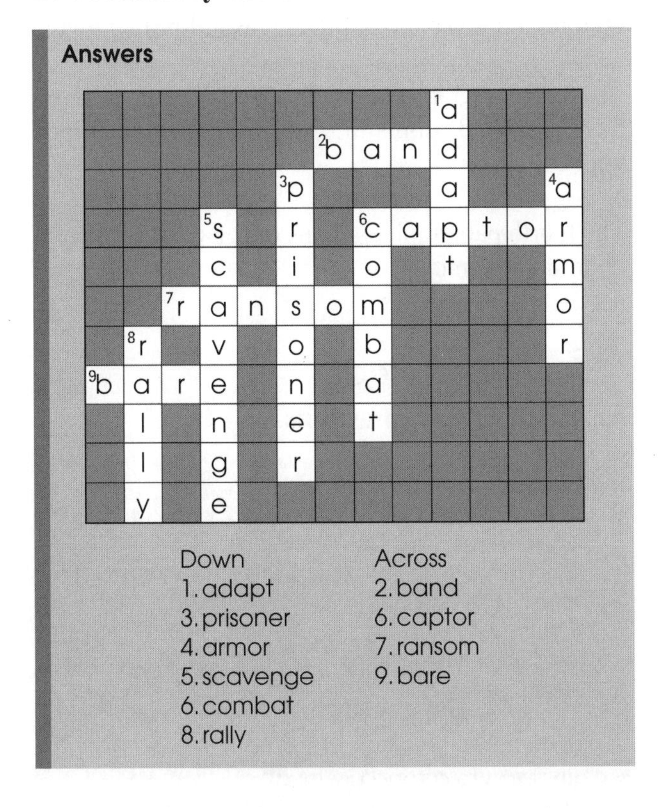

C. Choose the best answer.

Answers
1. b, 2. d, 3. c, 4. d, 5. b, 6. c, 7. d, 8. b, 9. d, 10. d

Review the cartoon

The cartoon shows a knight and his horse stuck in the mud up to their necks. His offer to sell the armor is too late. It's not good for anyone in this battle.

Teaching note

Students interested in learning more about the plays of Shakespeare in English can look up adaptations. The most famous of these are adaptations of twenty of the most popular plays by sister and brother, Charles and Mary Lamb, who first published their work in 1807. The collection has been popular ever since and is now freely available on the WWW.

Unit 10
The Future of Education

Fields of study:
Education, Computing

- Education is subdivided into many areas of study depending on the age and focus of each group, but it is generally concerned with the process of teaching and learning, usually at school, college or university. Education is an essential aspect of progress so the study of how to make education more effective is also essential.
- Computing is concerned with the use of computers in homes, schools and businesses. In the last fifty years, computing has become increasingly important and the study of computing has expanded to determine the best ways for people to work with computers.

Lesson One

Background information
This unit discusses the history of the ancient English university, Oxford, and the development of universities in Asia. The two readings discuss the history of ideas about education and show how they have merged today into common ideals.

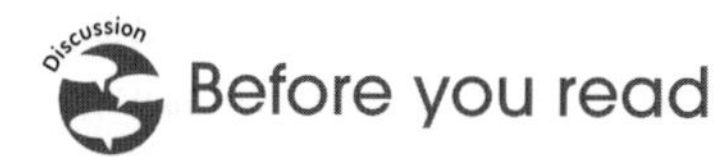

Before you read

Answers
- English-speaking universities have been around since 1096.
- Answers will vary, but the future of universities is probably moving towards greater flexibility in the ways in which subjects are taught as well as what subjects are taught.

What's happening in the pictures?
The pictures show various views of university life. Clockwise from top left: students working together in class, student working in a science lab, students graduating, students discussing a topic during a break.

Read about it

Answers
- Many people have a classic(al) image of what a university should look like.
- The special thing about Oxford University is that it is the first English-speaking university and set the traditions for many universities that followed.

An Ancient and Modern University

The passage talks about the nature of university education, using the history of Oxford University as an example.

The first paragraph describes the traditional image of the university. The second paragraph introduces Oxford and gives the political reason for its growth.

The third paragraph shows how the university evolved from scattered rooms in a town to its own campus with colleges.

The fourth paragraph explains the place of women at Oxford University.

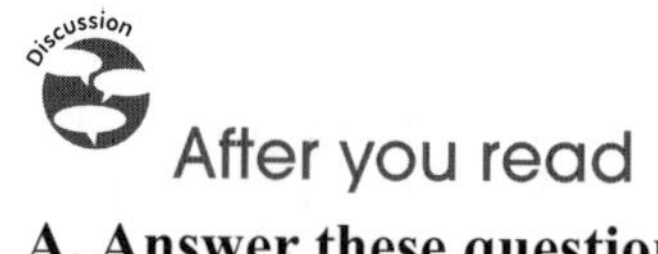

After you read

A. Answer these questions.

Answers
1. The "first" Oxford is famous for being the first English-speaking university.
2. Women were not allowed to attend Oxford for most of its history.
3. The term "town and gown" is popular probably because it is a clever description of differences that rhymes.
4. Henry II helped Oxford become more popular by banning English students from traveling outside England to attend university.
5. Universities invite international students to build up international relationships and expose their own students to new ways of thinking.

Reading strategy: Contractions

Contractions are common in informal spoken and written English. Students need to know how to recognize them and when to use them. Read through the explanation with students. Ask questions to make sure they understand. Explain the four tips and ask students for examples. Beware of students using contractions inappropriately, such as adding an apostrophe to *its* when it is being used as a possessive, e.g. *The dog lifts it's paw* should be *The dog lifts its paw*.

B. Rewrite the sentences, writing out the contractions.

Answers

1. A university must serve the public; it should not just be for the rich.
2. He is an expert and knows more about ants than anyone in the world.
3. You will need two things for university: an interest in learning and time to study.
4. I would have gone to university if I had done better in school.
5. There is only one rule to education: think.

C. Fill in the missing words.

Answers

A university is an **institution** of higher learning where students receive an education and are granted **degrees** based upon their individual course of studies. A university will usually grant **bachelor's degrees** and in many instances will also offer **master's degrees** and **doctorate** degree programs.

What other ways can you define a university? Think about what else a university does.

Answer

Answers will vary, but one example is: Universities are also important research centers.

Lesson Two

Read about it

Answers

- The main purpose of educating men was once to prepare them for government service.
- The role of Asian governments in educating their citizens was traditionally just the offering of tests. Students were responsible for learning on their own at established academies.

The Growth of Asian Universities

This article contrasts Asian universities to Western universities in the ways in which they evolved. Asian formal education systems started much earlier than their Western counterparts but eventually followed the Western model.

The first paragraph introduces the Latin influence on universities. *Corporation* was a name once used for early universities.

The second paragraph discusses the roots of the Asian education system and the third paragraph explains how the Chinese educational system evolved.

The fourth paragraph shows the move toward Western universities as the current model in Asia.

After you read

A. Summarize the main idea in one sentence.

Answer

Answers will vary, but one example is: People need to continue learning throughout their lives, even after getting a university degree.

B. Vocabulary check.

Answer

curriculum

C. Choose the best answer.

Answer

1. a, 2. d, 3. b, 4. b, 5. b, 6. c, 7. c, 8. c

Unit 11

Extinct!

Fields of study: Biology, Geography

- Biology is the scientific study of living things and how they work. Biology is often tied to other disciplines such as medicine. Discoveries in biology are often applied in medicine to the creation of new drugs.
- Geography teaches us about the relationships of people and things across space. It is a useful tool for examining changes and differences.

Lesson One

Background information

This unit looks at two points of view about the extinction of different species, including plants and animals. The first article is a pessimistic look at a theory which predicts serious consequences if related plants and animals die. The second article is more optimistic and notes that theory and observation are not the same thing.

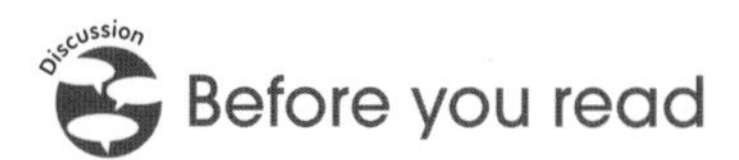

Answers
- Species become extinct because of changes to their environment or because they are displaced by other species.
- Extinctions affect us because it upsets the balance of helpful and hurtful species and may threaten us in terms of our food production.

What is happening in the pictures?

The pictures show stages of change from a jungle to an urban environment. Ask students about the changes and what changes they can relate from their own neighborhoods and experiences.

Answers
- A focus of this unit is how ideas are connected by prepositions.
- Islands provide a model for the impact of the extinction of a species.

Island Biogeography

This reading deals with a theory of how extinctions occur and how they affect other species.

The first paragraph identifies the problem of predicting a rate of extinction among animals, birds, insects and plants and a theory of two scientists.

The second paragraph explains the number of species found on an island as a balance between migration and extinction with five variables.

The third paragraph shows how the loss of one species affects others.

The fourth paragraph gives the impact of the scientists' theory but raises several criticisms.

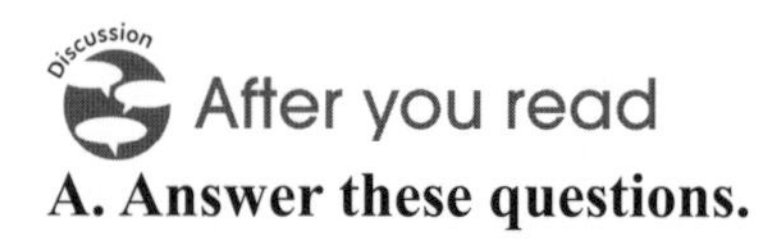

A. Answer these questions.

Answers
1. MacArthur and Wilson proposed their theory to predict the rate of extinction.
2. By "islands," they mean any area cut off from similar parts of nature. For example, an area of wilderness within a city or surrounded by farms.
3. A benefit of the theory has been the protection of many natural habitats.
4. If an island is not protected, MacArthur and Wilson suggest that one after another species will die as they are usually interdependent.
5. The term *biogeography* means the study of life over an area of land.

Reading strategy: Prepositions

Prepositions are generally small, short and common words, but they cause a lot of trouble for students because their use must be learned and general rules don't always apply. Read through the explanation with students. Ask questions to make sure they understand. Explain the four tips and ask students to collect examples of prepositions that they come across as they read.

B. Fill in the prepositions.

Answers
1. He was born **in** 1957 **on** April 1st.
2. My test is **on** Monday **at** another school.
3. We'll meet **in** Stanley Park **at** six o'clock.
4. He won the top spelling prize **in** our country **in** 2004.
5. **In** winter, we ski **at** a Korean resort.

C. Fill in the missing words.

Silent Spring is a book by Rachel Carson that describes how a **pesticide**, DDT, enters the **food chain** and **accumulates** in plants, insects and animals, including human beings, causing **cancer** and death. Carson found that DDT and other pesticides had **contaminated** the entire world food supply. DDT was eventually banned in the United States, but it is still produced there and sold in other countries.

In what other ways do we damage the environment?

Answer
Answers will vary, but one example is: The pollution we produce from driving cars damages the environment.

Lesson Two

Answers
- This article differs from the point of view of the article in Lesson One in that it challenges the theory with established facts.
- A fact is something which can be measured and is known to be true while an opinion is a subjective idea or belief about something.

How Many Species Become Extinct Each Year?

This article contrasts with the first article in that it provides facts that challenge the theory.

The first paragraph notes that people accept many ideas about species going extinct, but questions how these figures are arrived at.

The second paragraph gives the argument of the theory, but then the third paragraph challenges it with quotes by an economist who said that the world is actually improving.

The fourth paragraph explains that theory does not always match observation and, in fact, far fewer species may be disappearing.

Review the picture of the panda and ask students what other animals they know of facing extinction.

A. Summarize the main idea in one sentence.

Answer
Answers will vary, but one example is: Despite extensive deforestation and the loss of bird species in Puerto Rico in the 1900s, the number of bird species has actually been able to grow.

B. Vocabulary check.

Answer

R	D	W	R	A	U	S	I	E	S	J	I	R	F	V
L	E	A	X	E	Z	R	M	X	C	D	L	A	H	O
H	V	U	P	O	S	E	M	T	A	A	H	K	A	N
O	E	C	R	F	P	D	N	I	R	A	S	A	B	T
B	L	A	O	E	E	M	F	N	C	C	R	N	I	A
S	O	N	P	D	C	X	R	C	E	R	B	I	T	M
E	P	C	O	R	I	Q	A	T	T	P	S	I	A	I
R	M	E	S	C	E	E	F	I	S	E	O	H	T	N
V	E	R	E	C	S	C	I	O	P	S	S	P	S	A
A	N	D	C	Q	R	O	M	N	E	T	N	E	T	T
T	T	V	I	B	I	L	N	S	P	I	C	K	E	N
I	V	N	T	H	E	O	R	Y	I	C	M	I	E	D
O	N	J	G	R	L	G	U	G	E	I	C	C	O	E
N	E	W	H	Y	S	Y	E	V	S	D	E	N	R	G
R	E	S	O	U	R	C	E	S	C	E	M	A	Y	I

C. Choose the best answer.

Answers
1. a, 2. d, 3. c, 4. b, 5. a, 6. c, 7. c, 8. a

Review the cartoon

In the cartoon, a saber-toothed tiger is about to jump onto a confused scientist. While the scientist might normally be excited to find such an animal is not extinct, this isn't the best situation to discover it.

Teaching note

Whenever students take what they have learned in one way and use it in another form, it helps to reinforce learning. For example, reading about something and then speaking or writing about it helps to consolidate the ideas in their minds. Explain to students that they should always look for opportunities to reinforce their learning on their own.

Teaching note

Encourage students to keep a reading diary. They can write a short note about any piece of English they read that is longer than a page. It doesn't matter whether the reading is a novel or instructions. Ask students to share notes about what they read outside of class.

Unit 12
Angels or Outcasts?

Fields of study:
Psychology, Sociology, Medicine

- Psychology is the study of the mind and how it influences people's behavior. Psychology is important in many different fields where it is necessary to understand people's actions and reactions.
- Sociology is the scientific study of societies and the behavior of people in groups. Sociology is important in many other fields, such as business. For example, sociologists studying business may examine the ways in which people behave differently when in a group compared to how they act when they are alone.
- Medicine is the treatment and study of illnesses and injuries. Medicine is also tied to why people get sick and hurt themselves.

Lesson One

Background information

This unit looks at two points of view about how people change their looks with surgery. The first reading puts forward the opinion that changing your looks is both natural and advantageous. The second reading suggests that people who do so are freaks and that extreme cosmetic practices should be controlled by society.

Before you read

Answers
- You can permanently change your appearance by getting tattoos, scarring and inserting metal and bone pieces.
- It's a matter of personal opinion of what changes are and aren't OK, but a general principle is not to make changes that can interfere with your future. A tattoo on the lower back need not be seen in public on most occasions, but a tattoo on the face would interfere with being hired for many jobs. Some parents let their teenage children make changes as long as they are not permanent, e.g. temporary tattoos, changes to hair color and so on.

What's different about these people?

The people in the pictures have changed their appearances through tattoos and piercing, and inserting metal and bone objects in their tongues, ears and nostrils.

Read about it

Answers
- The title is a play on a common expression, usually used to compliment someone, e.g. "I love your hair!"
- The title suggests that the writer supports such plastic surgery.

I Love Your Wings!

This article is in favor of extreme forms of plastic surgery and explains how some of them would work.

The first paragraph introduces a plastic surgeon who believes people should be able to change their appearance in any way they want.

The second paragraph explains how new body parts are not unusual and gives examples.

The third paragraph shows how changes in plastic surgery are being made and how some people with extra fingers or thumbs might be capable of different jobs.

The fourth paragraph introduces a slight drawback: wings could not help you fly. But the paragraph also introduces the idea of body mapping that could help you control new limbs.

The fifth and final paragraph provides a thought-provoking idea about feeling better through plastic surgery.

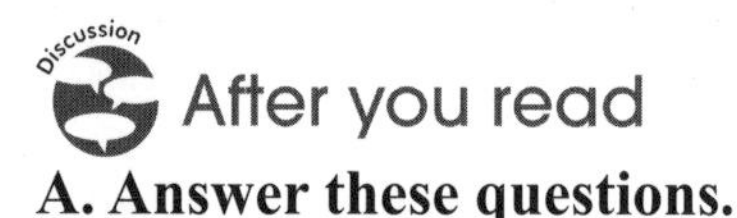

A. Answer these questions.

Answers

1. A person with wings would not be able to fly because human bones are too heavy compared to birds' hollow bones.
2. Dr. Rosen's usual job is a plastic surgeon.
3. Some people might want extra fingers to make them able to do new jobs or old jobs in different ways.
4. Different reasons for having plastic surgery are to look better or for medical reasons.
5. Many people have plastic surgery for medical reasons, to lose weight or to improve their appearance.

Reading strategy: Colons, em-dashes and semicolons

Like conjunctions, colons, em-dashes and semicolons are important to understanding and creating complex ideas. These bits of punctuation help to order ideas and show relationships between them. Read through the explanation with students. Ask questions to make sure they understand. Explain the four tips and ask students to look for examples of the punctuation as they read. Ask how changing the punctuation would change the meaning.

B. Add colons, em-dashes or semi-colons.

Answers

1. Plastic surgery just for beauty has a different name: cosmetic surgery.
2. Reasons for plastic surgery—not just for medical needs—are quickly changing.
3. Plastic surgery now has many uses: improving looks; losing weight; correcting physical problems.
4. No one knows what problems an operation may bring; be careful.
5. There are good reasons for changing the way we look: to feel better; to look younger; to lose dangerous weight.

C. Fill in the missing words.

Answers

Many people travel to have **diverse** kinds of plastic surgery. Such a trip can include a vacation and a less expensive operation. However, there can be many **complications**. First, you may not be able to **evaluate** the **qualifications** of the staff; they may not even be doctors. Second, the medical **facility** may not be safe. And third, you may need **extensive** follow-up care—which can be expensive back home—after your surgery. All in all, one should think cautiously about combining pleasure and surgery.

Lesson Two

Answers

- An outcast is someone who doesn't belong in the rest of society and has been sent away or "cast out."
- The title suggests the writer is not in favor of plastic surgery.

Making Outcasts

This article takes the opposite point of view of the first article and questions the reasons for people wanting to make themselves ugly with plastic surgery.

The first paragraph begins with an overview of plastic surgery, explaining its history.

The second paragraph shows how people's attitudes have changed from doing plastic surgery for medical reasons to doing it to make themselves ugly and animal-like.

The third paragraph suggests that the reasons for extreme plastic surgery is a mental problem that should be treated by psychiatrists.

Use the article and picture as a starting point to discuss plastic surgery.

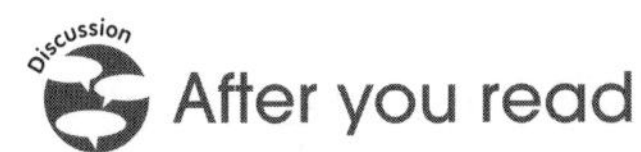

After you read

A. Summarize the main idea in one sentence.

Answer
Answers will vary, but one example is: Japanese tattoos have a long history based on power and fashion.

B. Vocabulary check.

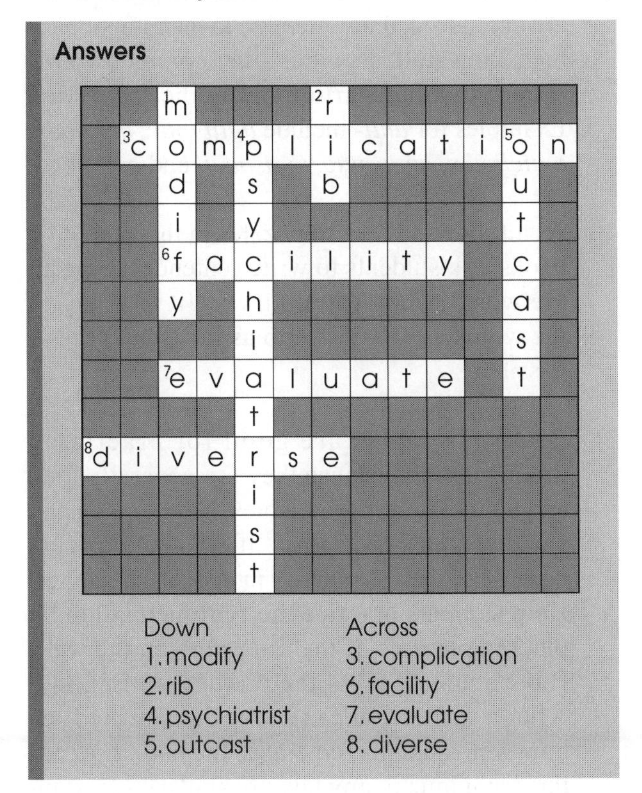

Down	Across
1. modify	3. complication
2. rib	6. facility
4. psychiatrist	7. evaluate
5. outcast	8. diverse

C. Choose the best answer.

Answers
1. a, 2. c, 3. d, 4. b, 5. a, 6. c, 7. b, 8. d

Teaching note

Ask students what process they go through when trying to decide which side of an argument they should support. Generally, it involves the following:

- listening or reading carefully;
- making sure that you understand both points of view;
- asking questions to clarify your understanding;
- comparing new information to what you knew before; and
- finally making a decision.

Teaching note

Help students with their pronunciation by asking them to read aloud. However, this is most effective (and less embarrassing) one-on-one.

Teaching Notes

1. To save yourself time, try different forms of peer editing. For example, after students have finished an exercise, put them in pairs to see if they agree on the answers. As they check each other's work, encourage them to give each other explanations in English for any corrections they might need. In time, you can adapt this technique to longer and more complicated tasks.

2. Make students responsible for what they study. As they finish each task and unit, remind them that they should understand the ideas completely. If not, it's their responsibility to reread, review and retry the tasks. A useful benchmark is the skills check on page 142 of the Student Book.

3. When students enjoy a particular activity, such as the logic problem on this page, direct them to further examples, such as a book on mazes in the library. Each reading should be a starting point for students to learn more about a topic.

4. Get an idea of who are the faster and slower readers by watching them as they read through the articles on their own. For the slower readers, you might privately suggest to them that they try reading ahead of each day's lesson. Also, emphasize that they need to pay particular attention to the reading strategies.

5. If student have access to the WWW, they can use the resources at www.read-and-think.com, but they can also search any topic that interests them. Turn students' questions in class to mini-assignments, asking students to find out a bit more and report back to class.

6. Bring cartoons to class with blanks in the speech and thought bubbles. It's a fun activity for students to add their own English text.

7. The exploration of space is often in the news and although students may know a lot about space, they probably do not know the names of the common planets, stars and space phenomena in English. Ask each student to "adopt a planet" or some other space phenomena and create a group poster on the wall with all the English vocabulary added.

8. Students often have difficulty reading novels and may need guidance. One way to help them is to introduce plot summaries, commonly available on the WWW, sometimes chapter by chapter. When students understand the general plot of a novel, it's easier for them to concentrate on the language they are reading and guess new vocabulary in context.

9. When common affixes, such as the prefix *anti-*, are introduced, draw attention to their importance by asking students what other common words they know that start or end in the same way. Examples for *anti-* include *antibiotic*, *antibody*, *anticlimax*, *antiseptic*, *antisocial* and *antithesis*.

10. As a follow-up idea to puzzles in this and other books, ask students to write sentences using all the words. They should try to fit as many of the words as possible into as few sentences as possible.

11. Dinosaur names are good for practicing pronunciation because they are generally long and feature multiple syllables. Moreover, many students know the names of certain dinosaurs because of their popularity in books and movies. Help students practice their pronunciation by placing pictures of the dinosaurs on the wall. Have students label the pictures in English. After a while, you can cover the labels to see how well students remember the names. Adapt this technique to any key vocabulary you want students to practice.

12. In every class, there are more able and less able students. Encourage them to help each other by arranging them in pairs. An important goal in teaching is to make sure that students are neither bored nor frustrated. Giving more able students a chance to help others is a good way to keep them happy and reinforce what they have learned.

13. Students interested in learning more about the plays of Shakespeare in English can look up adaptations. The most famous of these are adaptations of twenty of the most popular plays by sister and brother, Charles and Mary Lamb, who first published their work in 1807. The collection has been popular ever since and is now freely available on the WWW.

14. Whenever students take what they have learned in one way and use it in another form, it helps to reinforce learning. For example, reading about something and then speaking or writing about it helps to consolidate the ideas in their minds. Explain to students that they should always look for opportunities to reinforce their learning on their own.

15. Encourage students to keep a reading diary. They can write a short note about any piece of English they read that is longer than a page. It doesn't matter whether the reading is a novel or instructions. Ask students to share notes about what they read outside of class.

16. Ask students what process they go through when trying to decide which side of an argument they should support. Generally, it involves the following:
    - listening or reading carefully;
    - making sure that you understand both points of view;
    - asking questions to clarify your understanding;
    - comparing new information to what you knew before; and
    - finally making a decision.

17. Help students with their pronunciation by asking them to read aloud. However, this is most effective (and less embarrassing) one-on-one.